Center Field Grasses

Center Field Grasses

Poems from Baseball

GENE FEHLER

McFarland & Company, Inc., Publishers

Jefferson, North Carolina, and London

For Polly, Tim, and Andy,
with love

The present work is a reprint of the library bound edition of
Center Field Grasses: Poems from Baseball, *first published in
1991 by McFarland.*

LIBRARY OF CONGRESS CATALOGUING-IN-PUBLICATION DATA

Fehler, Gene, 1940–
       Center field grasses : poems from baseball / by Gene Fehler.
       p.   cm.

   ISBN 978-0-7864-6705-1
   softcover : acid free paper ∞

   PS3556.E37C46 2012
   811'.54 — dc20   90-53604

BRITISH LIBRARY CATALOGUING DATA ARE AVAILABLE

On the cover: Print titled *Our baseball heroes*, Richard K. Fox, ca.
1895, New York (Library of Congress); background image © 2012
Shutterstock

Manufactured in the United States of America

*McFarland & Company, Inc., Publishers
   Box 611, Jefferson, North Carolina 28640
   www.mcfarlandpub.com*

Acknowledgments

Grateful thanks are given to these publications, in which the following poems have appeared (several of them under different titles): *Alura:* "If God Were a Baseball Pitcher" (published as "A Response to Frost"); *Arulo!:* "He Might Even Win"; *Austin Poetry Sampler:* "Artificial Baseball," "Fielder's Mitt," "Rainy Night Baseball," "Two Outs and the Bases Loaded" (an excerpt from "Thirteen Ways of Looking at a Baseball Game"), "Two-Strike Bunt"; *Baseball Diamonds* (Doubleday): "Mel Stottlemyre"; *Baseball I Gave You All the Best Years of My Life* (North Atlantic Books): "Mel Stottlemyre"; *The Bedford Introduction to Literature* (St. Martin's): "To My Fans, on Becoming a Free Agent" (published as "If Richard Lovelace Became a Free Agent"); *Capper's Weekly:* "But I Was One-and-Twenty" (published as "If Housman Were a Batting Coach"), "The Curve Ball" (published as "If Tennyson Were a Junk Pitcher"), "Ebbets Field," "A Red-Faced Father"; *Circus Maximus:* "Contest Winner: June, 1955"; *Dream Writings and Scribbles:* "Old Autographs," "Shortstop, Making the Tag"; *English Journal:* "Tommy Hunter Tells Why He Was Kind to Walter Miller" (published as "First Pick"); *Green's Magazine:* "Error, Little League"; *The Inkling:* "On First Looking at a Mantle Homer," "Some Keep the Sabbath on the Mound"; *Jump River Review:* "Left-Handed Poetry"; *Late Knocking:* "Ever Reaching"; *Light Year '86* (Bits Press): "But I Was One-and-Twenty" (published as "If A.E. Housman Had Tried to Hit Big League Pitching"), "Grabbing an Illegal Bat at Yankee Stadium" (published as "If Billy Martin Managed the Yankees"), "To My Fans, on Becoming a Free Agent" (published as "If Richard Lovelace Became a Free Agent"); *The Minneapolis Review of Baseball:* "Artificial Baseball," "Fielder's Mitt," "The Philadelphia Three, Plus One," "Thirteen Ways of Looking at a Baseball Game"; *Muses Mill:* "Pitchers and Poets"; *The New York Times:* "Wilbur Wood"; *Nostalgia:* "Backyard Glory"; *Outerbridge:* "If

God Were a Baseball Pitcher" (published as "A Response to Frost"); *The Panhandler:* "Left-Handed Poetry"; *Pig Iron:* "The Cub Star," "Ebbets Field," "I Knew a Man Named Stengel" (published as "If e.e. cummings Followed Baseball"), "To Bunt, or Not to Bunt," "To My Fans, on Becoming a Free Agent" (published as "If Richard Lovelace Knew Baseball"); *Poultry—A Magazine of Verse:* "Artificial Grass," "Those Bases on Balls"; *Rockford Morning-Star:* "Mel Stottlemyre"; *The Rose's Hope:* "Backyard Glory"; *Southern Style:* "If Poets Were Baseball Players"; *Spitball:* "Backyard Glory," "The Bench-Warmer," "But I Was One-and-Twenty" (published as "I Heard a Wise Coach Say"), "Casey and the Agent," "Casey and the Dome," "The Chickenwirefence Behind My House," "Contest Winner: June, 1955," "Grabbing an Illegal Bat at Yankee Stadium" (published as "If Robert Frost Were Billy Martin"), "Hero," "If God Were a Baseball Pitcher," "I Keep the Sabbath on the Mound," "Left-Handed Pitcher," "Old Man Parker's Vacant Lot," "Sammy Cayson, Cucumbers, and Me," "Timeclock," "To Bunt, or Not to Bunt," "Wilbur Wood"; *Taurus:* "The Morning After"; *Voices International:* "Deathbed Showdown"; *Western Poetry Quarterly:* "Backyard Glory"; *Write On:* "Center Field Grasses"; *Writing Poems* (Little, Brown): "To My Fans, on Becoming a Free Agent" (published as "If Richard Lovelace Became a Free Agent"); *Yesterday's Magazine:* "Winner."

Table of Contents

Part Two: Parodies from the Classics

Part Three: The Players

Preface

"In the country of baseball, time is the air we
breathe, and the wind swirls us backward and forward,
until we seem so reckoned in time and seasons that
all time and all seasons become the same."
—Donald Hall, *In the Country of Baseball*, 1976

The beauty of baseball is that it is never "out of season." From
World Series to spring training is a time of recollections, and it is
a time of anticipation. The watcher of baseball captures moments
of time, encapsulates them to store up and to feed on in the dark
of winter when all the senses are yearning for the return of baseball
season. For the beginning of baseball season will bring with it the
discovery of new moments, new images that can be filed in
memory with the countless images already living there. To the fan,
baseball is truly, like a Wordsworth poem, "the spontaneous
overflow of powerful emotion recollected in tranquility."

The poems in this book share some moments that have been
lovingly engraved in my memory. They range from experiences
from my own childhood to re-creations of moments familiar to
most fans: Lou Gehrig standing before the microphone for his
"luckiest man" speech in 1939, Bobby Thomson circling the bases
after his 1951 "shot heard round the world," Willie Mays making
his over-the-shoulder catch and turning and throwing with his
cap flying off in the 1954 World Series, Dale Mitchell taking
the called third strike in Don Larsen's perfect game in the 1956
World Series, Jimmy Piersall running the bases backwards, Rocky
Colavito pointing his bat at the pitcher before the pitch.

The moments of baseball began for me when I was seven,
growing up in Thomson, a small Illinois town. My dad, a White
Sox fan, had spent this particular afternoon listening to their game
on the radio. I happened to enter the room in the last of the ninth.
Seeing Dad's excitement, I stopped to listen. The Sox trailed by

one run. Bases loaded. Two out. Floyd Baker, the Sox third baseman, at bat. As the count ran to three and two I began to share Dad's excitement. After more than two hours of setting the stage, it had all come down to one pitch — a strike or a ball, a hit or an out. I realized for the first time the dramatic purity of baseball. Baker, if memory serves, went out to end the game. But what he did was not important. I realized even then that the important thing was the anticipation, the thrill of exploring the possibilities of all the things that could happen.

From that moment, I became hopelessly devoted to baseball. Along with Lew Frosch and Johnny Creighton, I spent most of my waking hours playing it; I spent practically all my waking night-time hours with a set of dice, playing APBA baseball and baseball games of my own invention. The most pleasant part of the school year was the baseball season with its afterschool practices and games, but even in the off season I found time at school for baseball. Bill Feddersen and I would often go to the vacant typing room at old Thomson High during our free period, take out a pair of dice ("duce," we called them), and play a game we designed, usually with the Cardinals (Bill's favorite) against my Yankees.

Bill, whose own childhood love of baseball obviously prepared him well for his career as a college president, showed that he understood how important baseball was to me when he closed his remarks in my high school yearbook like this:

> Gene ... You're a pretty good ball player and I hope you get a chance to play in the minors before you start teaching, because I know if you get in the majors you won't teach. Hang on to your "duce" and keep figuring "statics."

Well, I didn't make the minors (how many of us do?), and I did end up teaching for many happy years. Throughout those years, baseball has remained a priority. Yes, I have managed to hang on to my "duce" and have kept figuring "statics."

I began to write baseball poetry while teaching English and creative writing at Kishwaukee College in Malta, Illinois. I owe a debt of gratitude to my friend, colleague, and fellow baseball-trivia buff Vance Barrie for his encouragement and support.

During my eleven years at Kishwaukee College, I discovered that baseball and poetry were made for each other. Each swing of the bat, each headfirst slide, each moment the ball slaps into the glove is a poem. Analogously, in just a few lines the poet says to us, "Here is a moment in time. I want to share it with you. Take it. Look at it. Experience its beauty or sadness or joy."

Dylan Thomas said of poetry, "All that matters is the enjoyment of it." That is the premise of this book. Enjoy whatever you want in these poems — their sounds, their words, their moments, their people, their emotions. Baseball poems are largely intended for at least two groups of readers: fans of baseball and lovers of poetry. Even if you do not fall into either group, there is a good chance you will find much of interest on these pages.

To many of our best writers, baseball has been the tapestry on which is painted life itself. In the best of the "baseball novels" (*The Natural, Bang the Drum Slowly, Shoeless Joe, The Universal Baseball Association, The Conduct of the Game, The Celebrant*), the people and the feelings are most important. Yet even those readers who do not follow the game closely can enjoy good baseball literature. Lovers of poetry and baseball fans will both find pleasure in magazines like *Spitball* and *The Minneapolis Review of Baseball*, quarterly small press publications filled with sparkling baseball poems by such talented poets as R.L. Keyes, Jim Palana, Tim Peeler, Mike Shannon, Alan Catlin, Phillip Darcy, Jim Daniels, Ken Lazebnik, Virgil Smith, Daniel Martin, David Holdt, R.L. Harrison, Earl Butler, Jan Brodt, Major Ragain, Tom Sheehan, and many others.

It would be impossible to list the names of all the well-known poets who have been inspired by baseball. Such a list would, however, surely include Tom Clark, Marianne Moore, Donald Hall, Richard Hugo, Fred Chapell, Robert Francis, Robert Wallace, William Packard, Stephen Cormany, Rolph Humphries, Merritt Clifton, Kenneth Patchan, and Lillian Morrison.

This list of baseball poets is far from complete. Many readers will spot significant omissions. Nevertheless, the length of this incomplete list should make one thing clear, however: baseball has inspired thousands of poems. Some write about baseball because it is mythic or because it is a metaphor for life. Many write because of the universal experiences and emotions the world of baseball provides. Most write because they love baseball.

Part One: Up Close and Personal

I have arranged my baseball poems in three sections: "Up Close and Personal," "Baseball Parodies," and "The Players." In the first section, "Up Close and Personal," you will likely see yourself at times, perhaps as a youngster on the playing field, or as a parent sharing a baseball moment with a child, or as a grown-up, trying to stay young.

Or maybe you will see yourself in the reflection of attitudes. (Especially if you are a baseball "purist" and prefer parks like Wrigley and Fenway.) In my poem "Artificial Baseball" the fan in the 1990s

> Stood watch outside the massive sterile dome
> Where air-conditioned artificial turf
> Took weary time-warped players far from home

Yet many of us prefer the time when

> Past summers, with their breeze-filled victories,
> Lit up the parks where players learned to read
> The speed of sky, twist of cloud, slant of sun—
> The language that they knew they all would need.

Those of you who have spent hours (especially in winter) with your dice or at the computer, making up line-ups and schedules and keeping statistics for your own league, might feel as I did in my poem "Dice Baseball":

> It's not enough, the news of swaps.
> I need base hits on table tops
> where I will stuff desserts away—
> those feasts of baseball, night and day.
> . . . .
> For all true fans I stake my claim:
> Dice Baseball is "The Winter Game."

Dice games helped get me through the winter. But I wasn't alone in wanting spring to come. My ball glove wanted it as well. My first glove was an oversized first baseman's mitt that my friends all called the "bushel basket." My poem "Fielder's Mitt" describes how my glove felt when it was

> stiff from winter's bench-
> warming cold,

Many a winter day I took my mitt off the shelf, knowing that it

> waits for spring,
> for mud-scuffed balls
> slapping past, taunting
> "Catch me if you can!"

Even if you cannot remember your first mitt, I suspect that at one time or another you have played baseball. If not in an organized league, at least in a pick-up game or in gym class. And almost everyone who has played can identify with the boy in "Error, Little League" who

> dropped the ball
> that, caught, would have
> made him a hero in eyes
> now glinting steel

or if you're lucky, you'll identify with the hero in "Winner":

> what I remember most
> is my dad behind the rusted screen
> back of home plate
> "You can hit this guy!"

As important as baseball was in my childhood, it's been no less important since. Those of you who are trying to keep up with your sons (or daughters) might feel as I did in "Backyard Glory":

> I will have to bear down
> as middle age nears,
> to convince him that I'm still
> the best pitcher around.

Or maybe you can share the regret of the narrator of "Center Field Grasses," who returns to his old ballfield:

> Beneath my feet on center field grasses
> where once I roamed free
> and with abandon
> slid on a hard belly of youth
> to catch line drives,
> now cattle munch,
> unaware of history.

While he is reminiscing, his sons in the car try to rush him:

> I let them honk.
> I turn my back to them,

fighting tears,
cursing silently,
wishing I could go back
to voices from long ago,
because my sons are in a hurry:
they don't know who I am.

I feel fortunate that my own sons "know who I am," and that at almost fifty I was able to play with them on the same church softball team and engage in a friendly competition for batting honors (an experience descibed in "After Being Outhit by My Sons").

Baseball is one of the best ways to bring families together. In "Deathbed Showdown" the father, dying, recalls a moment years ago when his son's double won a baseball game:

"You came through, Son! You came through."
The son squeezes his father's hand,
knows the end is imminent....

The beauty of baseball is that even though we do not always "come through," there is always the anticipation that we will.

Part Two: Baseball Parodies — Poems from the Classics

The poems in this section can serve a dual purpose: they can, on their own, bring us pleasure, yet they can also lead us into a reading of the classics. In the poems in this section, you'll hear the sounds and rhythms of Robert Frost and Emily Dickinson and Edgar Allan Poe. You'll recognize the forms and typography of Cummings and Ferlinghetti and Whitman. The fifty-nine parody poems imitate the form and style of thirty-eight famous poets.

We read first for pleasure; that should go without saying. But of special value, especially in a school setting, will be for the reader to move from the parody to the original. (Or to move from the original to the parody.) Whereas Robert Frost ("Mending Wall") describes a farmer who "doesn't love a wall," my version ("Those Bases on Balls") describes a manager who "doesn't love a ball," especially when it leads to a base on balls:

The walks I mean,
No manager can bear to see them made,
But almost every game I see them there.
I meet my pitcher out upon the hill
When all the bases have been filled by walks

And start to send him to the showers once again.
He keeps the ball and will not let it go.

Oliver Wendell Holmes spoke of the proposed breaking up of
the U.S. frigate *Constitution* in "Concord Hymn": "Ay, tear her tat-
tered ensign down!" My "Ebbets Field" narrator talks of the pro-
posed destruction of the old home of the Brooklyn Dodgers:

Don't tear the treasured ballpark down!
Long has it brought me joy. . . .

We can read here of "all those enduring old arms" (pitchers
like Phil Niekro, Tommy John, Nolan Ryan, Hoyt Wilhelm — all
pitching successfully well into their forties). Then we can turn to
Thomas Moore's famous poem and hear the same sounds as he
speaks to us of "all those endearing old charms."

Shakespeare's Hamlet explores the question "To Be, or Not to
Be." My version shows a manager exploring a key question of
strategy: "To Bunt, or Not to Bunt":

Whether 'tis safer in the end to challenge
The arm of a hard-charging third baseman
Or to try slashing a line drive past him,
And in the process end him?

If we enjoy Tennyson's wonderful poem "The Charge of the
Light Brigade," we might also find pleasure in "The Charge of the
Mighty Wade," describing Boston Red Sox third baseman Wade
Boggs' attempt to reach the coveted .400 mark in hitting:

Line drives to the right of them,
Line drives to the left of them,
Line drives far over them
Rattled and thundered;

If we, as baseball fans, enjoy the parodies, we will certainly
enjoy the classics on which the parodies are based.

If we, as lovers of poetry, enjoy the classics, we should also
find pleasure in the parodies, even if we don't have all of the pas-
sion of the baseball devotee.

Part Three: The Players

The eighty-seven poems in the final section focus on the lives
or singular moments in the careers of individual players.

Maybe you'll recognize one or more of your favorite players in this section. Some are easily recognizable:

> Quick wrists and "It's a great day to play two!"
> and baseball became a game again.

or

> High Heat
> that once struck out
> 20 in a game

Some may be less obvious, like the player who was

> waived out of the league
> by that frozen Idaho lake.

or the pitcher we respected for the wrong reasons:

> Unknowing fans throught him a hero;
> knowing fans know him a hero
> who stopped crawling in the dust.

Most will recall three Philadelphia pitchers — Bobby Shantz, Curt Simmons, Robin Roberts. We can see them now with Jack Brown in "The Philadelphia Three, Plus One," a golfing foursome

> to whom the tiny, flagged hole cut from the narrow green
> beyond the fairway bunkers, water, and tree-lined rough
> must seem as menacing as Mantle or Williams
> or the Duke or Stan the Man
> or Willie waving lumber sixty feet away.

Many of the players are household names. I expect that most readers will have heard more than passing mention of Hank Aaron, Stan Musial and Sandy Koufax. However, even the most avid fan might not be able to give detailed accounts of the careers of Gavvy Cravath, Paul Giel, Harry Agganis, or Gary Kolb.

As you read these poems, my hope is that they will stir some memories or emotions in you. Perhaps you will be inspired to write a poem of your own in which you describe a moment in the career of one of your favorite players. Above all, enjoy.

Gene Fehler, Spring 1991, Seneca, South Carolina

Part One:
Up Close and Personal

Backyard Glory

Our Yankee Stadium:
the October cornfield-bordered
backyard diamond where my son
with teeth clenched
squeezes the bat,
waiting for my smoke.
I fire Koufax-quick
toward the bat lashing out;
the ball flies toward the apple tree
behind where my second baseman
would be if our yard
sprouted second basemen
as easily as dandelions;
it clears the tree and the fence
and drops into Indian summer's
dried corn stalks,
crackling like the explosive cheers
of bleacher fans.
Leaves spin like confetti
to honor his longest home run
in four years of batting against me.
I will have to bear down
as middle age nears,
to convince him that I'm still
the best pitcher around.

Fielder's Mitt

On the shelf my mitt,
stiff from winter's bench-
warming cold,
waits for spring,
for mud-scuffed balls
slapping past, taunting
"Catch me if you can!"
a challenge
that thaws my mitt
for a chase
through any mud-warmed ballpark
in suddenly
spring.

Old Autographs

Wrigley Field Sunday,
me near the railing
by front row boxes
like I belonged there,
yet fearing an usher's
"Time's up!"
while heroes
too large to touch
made gifts of their names

five in all,
scrawled by pitchers' hands
curving around the pen,
searching for seams —
catchers' gnarled hands as steady
as a snap throw to first —
hands of singles hitters
choking up on the pen
for control

and now:
the yellowing paper,
half-forgotten names penned
by hands that discovered
other things to touch,
softer things maybe,
like a waiting wife's cheek,
or the hands of a child
almost grown

Sleeping Over

We shared a bed that summer night
when we were fifteen.
Johnny and I stripped to our jockey shorts,
fought the push of July heat with root beer
half-frozen to crystal slush in iced mugs
while static from a bedside radio
screamed of strikeouts and singles.

At midnight, the Cardinal game over,
we slipped into cutoff shorts.
In the back yard, beneath the glare
of 60 watts, we threw popups to each other,
sharing laughter with crickets
as we dodged wasp-sized mosquitos
in a futile try to catch shadows.

Then we slept through the night,
dreaming of home runs and diving catches,
unashamed of our near nakedness,
unaware that a future world might raise eyebrows
at the sight of us side by side, almost touching
in the too sudden passing hours
of our innocence.

Contest Winner, July, 1955

I showed the postcard from Dell's
Baseball Annual contest to my buddies.
They took turns reading it:
"Congratulations! . . . Your autographed
baseball should reach you shortly."
Names paraded in my head: Berra,
Spahn, Williams, Musial, Mays.
Perhaps they would have a great from
the past: Cobb, Ruth, Tris Speaker,
maybe even "The Iron Horse"—Gehrig.
I cleared a permanent spot on my dresser,
a throne for that sacred name.
It would reign secure; no grass
would stain it, no dirt scuff it.

When the day came, I phoned my buddies.
Fingers trembling, we opened the package
together. Neat blue script on white leather.

Jake Pitler.

Jake Pitler?
I ran for my *Encyclopedia of Baseball:*
PIPP, WALTER CLEMENT
PIPPEN, HENRY HAROLD (Cotton)
PITKO, ALEXANDER
then! . . .
PITLER, JACOB ALBERT
b. April 22, 1894, at New York, N.Y.
1917 Pittsburgh NL 2B 109 .233
1918 Pittsburgh NL 2B   3 .000

Johnny was the first to laugh;
within seconds we had all joined in.
Jake Pitler.
One hundred twelve games in the bigs,
almost forty years ago.
Within a week, we had knocked the cover off.

Error, Little League

he dropped the ball
and the sky fell;
cats doused in gasoline
could not have sent screams
cutting toward him
so loud, so painful

he dropped the ball
into the dust
where it will blow
around in the attic
of his memory, mixing with
curses of coaches and parents

he dropped the ball
that, caught, would have
made him a hero in eyes
now glinting steel in some
faroff world beyond that wall
called the first base line

A Father's Dreams

The youthful image grins with eyes
Too young for sin, still full of trust,
From faded dog-eared photographs
Now dim like windows glazed with dust.

The son had slammed a home run once
Beneath the pride of Father's gaze
From splintered bleachers which, like dads,
Had once known younger, better days.

The son, now scornful of such games,
Has buried past loves with a sneer
Beneath accumulated trips
Of sex and acid, grass and beer.

The father lives through memories:
That last home run is magnified.
A faded photo catches tears
Of mourning for the dreams that died.

Two-Strike Bunt

Bouncing,
Skidding,
Wavering,
Sliding,
The ball fights the line
Like a frightened tightrope walker.
It watches frozen fielders,
Clings to chalked edges,
Stretches toward third base's shadow,
Then,
Inches from safety,
Somersaults into foul ground's
Netless doom.

Sammy Cayson, Cucumbers, and Me

Cayson's cucumber patch
watched us warm up,
yawned through the July sun,
and swallowed my only baseball.
Sammy and I stomped in,
ripped at its throat,
plowed through its perfect camouflage,
searched in vain for the
brown-green ball.

"My cucumber patch!"
Mrs. Cayson flew through the back door,
catching up with her words.
Tears clanked against her narrow face.
Her skinny fingers lashed out.
I sprinted from the tearing sound
of Sammy's blue t-shirt.
I was halfway down the alley
when the ball thudded behind me.

It rolled, cool as a cucumber,
at my feet. I glanced back,
saw her, a seething scarecrow,
gripping her throwing arm.
I told Allan Cook, our catcher, who,
for seven innings next game, chattered:
"Fire the old cucumber in, Sammy!"
Sammy wouldn't show us a single smile,
even though he no-hit the son-of-a-guns.

Scouting Reports

Gramps, you said you weren't going to die
until you saw me in the Big Leagues.
(We should both be so lucky.)
But some vows we have no control over.
You watched me through a grandfather's glasses;
pro scouts watched me through clinical eyes.

The Big Leagues survived without me.
I was twenty-one when you died,
twenty years ago, but I still see you leaning back
in your favorite chair, ear pressed to the radio,
listening for the call: "Banks to Baker to Fondy!
The Cubs turn two! The ball game is over!"

I imagine you are still sitting, eyeing scouting reports,
radio at your ear, as St. Peter calls the action.
You listen for my name, for the game-saver,
or, at least, for the steady performance.
I'm trying hard as I can, Gramps,
to keep from disappointing you again.

My First Baseball Cards

My first five basball cards:
Lou Brissie, Sid Hudson, Gil Coan,
Johnny Lindell, Johnny Hopp.
My mother found them in bubble gum,
gave them for my eighth birthday.
She told me they were baseball's best.

Worn from touching, the cards bent
from being carried in my back pocket
while I threw against the plank fence
behind the house, practicing to be
another Brissie or Hudson,
baseball's top pitchers.

I took practice swings, imitating
sluggers Coan, Hopp, Lindell.
Years later I checked their totals:
Lou and Sid won 148, lost 200.
Johnny L., Gil, and Johnny H.
batted .277 with 2,755 for 9,932.

No matter. Those five idols
who made my Hall of Fame
back when it was as large as my world
will never have their election
overturned by something as trivial
as a row of numbers.

In October

Damp hangs like a curtain
over the stadium,
empty in the aftermath.

My spirit droops now
after three days soaring—
the champagne, the parades,
the cheers, celebrations
funneled now into memories.

Rows of seats stare unseeing,
blinded by the gray cover
of coming winter.

Grass sags, knows that fall's
frozen football bodies
follow the baseball ballet,
the October orchestra
whose World Series music
softens, saddens me
in the sweetness of its finale.

The curtain closes on a stage
lonely and barren
until spring's standing ovation.

If Poets Were Baseball Players

At the arbritration hearing my agent pled my case:
"A hundred bucks for twenty poems? An absolute disgrace!
Just look at all the similes; they're worth a hundred each.
His symbols, subtle yet profound, both entertain and teach.

"Alliteration? Sixteen times. At least twelve metaphors.
His rhyme's exact. His rhythm? — well, it bounces, never bores.
In free verse, blank verse, villanelle, he's certainly a master.
In sonnets he's Bill Shakespeare's match, and my man writes them faster.

"John Milton, Shelley, Frost and Poe wrote poems quite second rate
Beside the masterpieces that we've seen my client create.
In summary, just let me say, the editor's unfair;
an athlete with less talent soon becomes a millionaire."

"Perhaps," the editor replied. "But surely you'll agree
that throughout history most poets wrote their poems for free.
They believed that wealth would just corrupt; they wrote for love of art.
So what's this talk of athletes? Why, the two are world's apart.

"A poem's a poem. It's only words few people want to read.
It isn't tension like when Sutter's clinging to a lead.
It's not a home run ball that's fought for by some screaming fans
that pay good money for the right to drink beer in the stands.

"But most of all, the bottom line is this: poems just don't sell,
especially if they're profound, or if they're written well.
Oh, sometimes drivel hits the charts, some hackwork best forgotten.
Most money-making poems, I fear, poetically are rotten."

The arbitrator mused aloud, "That's all I need to know."
He then said to the editor, "Ten thousand's what you owe."
My pride has suffered from a thought that's really rather chilling:
if quality won't sell, then why did my poems make a killing?

Rainy Night Baseball

sky of rain diamonds
flung beneath a bank of lights:
damp jeweled splendor

After Being Outhit by My Sons

"Softball is symbolic," my wife says, tossing names
at me: Ponce de Leon, Golden Fleece, Eldorado
and Holy Grail—to describe my nothing-less-than frantic

rush through outfield grasses chasing down deep fly balls.
"Softball is fun, that's all," I reply, thinking
especially of our competition for batting honors—

my sons and me, playing on the same team.
Like last night when Tim and Andy, the college boys,
bagged three hits each; I, the old-timer, got two.

Little difference, except theirs were for power:
line drives—two singles, two doubles, triple, home run;
mine: two bloop singles. As through a rainbowed lens

I see myself at the top of a mountain,
sliding inevitably toward bottom—yet with a clear view
of Tim and Andy scaling the steep slope.

"Softball is fun," I repeat,
yet do not speak of mountains to my wife,
who looks everywhere for symbols.

Chocolate Malteds

Curt couldn't throw his drop ball
with two strikes.
Coach's orders.
Not with Slow Motion Martin
behind the plate
dreaming of pizza and chocolate malteds.

Breaking pitches had a knack
for missing Martin's mitt,
so Curt stuck with the fast ball,
only whiffed fifteen a game
instead of the twenty he might have had.
Curt didn't mind.

In the dugout, we rose as one
when Slow Motion Martin swung.
Opponents thought him too pitiful
to waste a walk on. Their cries,
"Easy out!" caught in their throats
like dried bones of turkeys.

He took forever rounding the bases.
The bench sagged in the center
when he plopped back down.
We didn't mind.
We all bought him chocolate malteds
whenever he asked.

When the Hurt Begins

"You'll never get hurt working. I'll bet on it,"
Mom said time and time again, after the spiking
and the eight stitches above my left knee,
after the broken collarbone chasing the line drive
into the center field fence, after the concussion
from diving into an errant pick-off throw at first.
She never understood that my pain wasn't from injuries;
pain was from missing a game or two, or, that one time,
from missing six weeks from a broken bone. Most of all,
though, pain was from not being good enough, from
watching thousands of less dedicated ballplayers
make the big time, while I watched on tv and dreamed
of how it must be to play against the best.

"You'll never get hurt working," Mom said, patching cuts,
but she was wrong. She measured hurt in blood and bruises.
She would never understand that I hurt every day,
April through October, watching through my office window
the sun shining on the tattered ballfield down the block
where kids sometimes shout away summer afternoons.
On a slow day, or when the boss is gone, I close
my eyes against the urgency of now, and remember
those days of reckless abandon, of glorious yearning.
It seems only yesterday I was indestructible. Now
I hurt evenings, spreading my briefcase before beer
commercials made by retired superstars, old idols,
and I often wonder if they hurt just as much as I.

Dice Baseball

October outdoor action ends,
and while my heart (the Cubs lost) mends,
I'll bring out all my treasured dice.
The Hot Stove League will not suffice
to take me all the way to spring.
I need the joy my dice can bring.

The contract talks, free agency,
are not enough pure sport for me.
It's not enough, the news of swaps.
I need base hits on table tops
where I will stuff desserts away —
those feasts of baseball, night and day.

The choice of games that I can see
Is not dictated by tv.
I'll give the Cubs a chance, or two,
to win the league before I'm through.
For all true fans I stake my claim:
Dice baseball is "The Winter Game."

Shortstop, Making the Tag

I like   the crowd's
the quiet   roar
of   and an umpire's
infield dust,   loud
rising   shout:
in a cloud   "OUT!"
beneath

Rain Delay

Players scatter beneath the flood.
Half of a giant centipede scurries toward center field,
painting the ground green behind it.

Raindrops bubble on the green;
they sit in puddles while box seat umbrellas blossom
like finger-painted toadstools.

One inning short of losing, the visitors dance
rain-dances behind water cascading from the dugout roof
like a dropped fly ball.

The home team throws curses
to the black thunder; umpires phone either
the weather bureau or God.

Broadcasters search for warm bodies
and fluid tongues to fill the airways with dripping words
of professional time-killers.

Players return to the clubhouse
where gin rummy cards flip from fingers like sure-
handed infielders turning a double play.

Box scores are seen on faces;
Hits washed out never make the newspapers,
count for nothing at contract time.

Rain Delay, the Aftermath

The ground crew pulls behind them
tons of water, forming a lake where fly balls
will sink into doubles, skip into triples.

Cheering fans seep out
from the grandstand roof like ants from beneath
a cake-sprinkled picnic blanket.

The visitors, trailing, forced now
to play their way to defeat, walk with the stiffness
of inactivity onto the field.

They wish that the aftermath
of the flood had left either a rainbow
to look at or an olive branch to grasp.

The home team frolics on the field
like ten-year-olds through Mom-forbidden
depths of spring puddles.

They do not know that the game
they think is all but over has been irretrievably lost
behind the tent flap of history.

Or that what awaits their tentative
shouts across the quagmire is nothing more
than the first hint of a beg/inning.

Strawberries

The umpire called me out,
else the strawberry
that has me sleeping
on my left side
would be no more painful
than a mosquito bite.

But I was out
sliding home
to end the game
one run down,
and I toss all night
trying to ease the pain.

I keep awake my wife
of twenty-five years
who thinks I play ball
only to deny my age.
"You deserve it, old man,"
she says. "Don't be a baby."

I was out, but next week
more strawberries wait
on the basepaths
for the opportune time
to leap at sliding old men
who age only in body.

Summer Paradise: Yankees, 1956

MM

EH   HB

F
ordSk
owronMart
inMcDougaldCa
reyBerraKucksLars
enSturdivantTurleyByr
neRColemanJColemanGrimM
organCollinsSeibernCerv
LumpeRizzutoNoren
McDermottSlau
ghterandS
tenge
l

T   t
  h   l
    e   i
H   u
     o   B
   useThatRuth

Sunday Evening

A kid, seven or eight,
I spent Sunday afternoons
as bat boy for the Thomson Merchants,
watched my dad play — an outfielder,
he could catch balls hit so high
the clouds seemed to swallow them
then spit them back twice as hard
and so far from him he had to race
faster than God to catch them.
And he did, every one.

After supper, win or lose,
with the town as still as a painting
and the sky a silent purple,
we'd walk through thoughts of afternoon's magic
to Joe Mack's Phillips '66 station.
Only occasional cars stopped by.
The men just sat around, four or five of them,
all my dad's age or older.
I watched them talk without really hearing
their words, without caring what they said.

What I remember most is the silence between stories,
their smiles, the smoke from their cigarettes,
the purple of sky, the silence of the Sunday street,
the half-repaired cars inside, waiting for Monday.
My dad, big and powerful and handsome,
would buy me a bottle of root beer
from the red cooler. I'd shake it up,
hold my thumb over the opening
until the bottle filled with foam.
I'd suck it down coolly.

Then, behind the station I'd find a stick
and hit bottle caps toward rows of junked cars —
the Chevy: a single,
the scattering of old Fords: outs,
the Studebaker: a walk,
the Packard: a home run —
until the purple paled
as night fell silently and Dad came out
to give me his powerful hand to hold
while he walked me home.

Tommy Hunter Tells Why
He Was Kind to Walter Miller

At recess I was always picked first
for baseball
back in fifth grade.
I was biggest,
could hit farther than anyone
except Mr. Lumas,
who taught gym.

Walter Miller, the slowest, clumsiest,
most picked on, was picked last,
stuck always in right field
where almost no one hit, except me
who, every time,
drove the ball toward Walter,
through him, over him.

Too often, the jeers would send Walter home.
I always begged him to stay.
I knew an easy home run when I saw it,
and didn't relish the thought
of someone catching my drives,
of my sometime not being
picked first.

Throwing It Back

He caught it
barehanded
350 feet from where it struck
Murphy's bat
and exploded into
three Atlanta runs.

Diehard bleacher fans,
Cub fans all,
accept no part
of an enemy's home run.
"Throw it back! Throw it back!"

He hesitated. This catch of his,
his first in years of waiting, hoping.
Fulfillment of a dream.

"Throw it back!"
A hundred fingers pointed
toward the fence.

The deed done,
he sank to his seat,
stared at his hands,
hands that fashioned a marvelous catch,
hands now
empty.

Karl Bailey's Ground Rule

Leaping for the game-winning home run,
Milledgeville's right fielder
split his chest across the barbed wire.
His white uniform spit red.
It took sixty stitches to hold him together,
to teach him to shy from fences.

Bailey owned the devil fence that separated
his grazing pasture from our high school's
right field. Even after the lawsuit was settled,
Bailey refused to sell his pasture.
And when he took the barbed wire out,
he set up his own ground rule:

a "No Trespassing" sign, complete with threats
of lawsuits of his own. Next season, Coach banned
our left-handed sluggers from batting practice.
Still, by midseason baseballs and cattle dung
sprang up like land-mines in "no man's land,"
the half-grazed grass of Bailey's forbidden pasture.

Line-Up

catcher
leather hands
        fingers webbed beneath
    doorknob knuckles

            pitcher
lover's fingers
        caress curve of seams
        mastering mistresses

first baseman
lumberjack legs:
        pointers for stretching
    alligator hand

        second baseman
hummingbird hands
            capture shadows
    to wrap in ribbons

        third baseman
jaguar quick
            leaping for darters
    on dancing feet

        shortstop
yardstick fingers
            strong, flexible
    dangle on bullwhip arm

        outfielders
midsummernight elves
            snatch fireflies
    in arc-lit twilight

Pitchers and Poets

A pitcher, like a poet, hurls the ball
Deceptively across the hitter's zone.
He changes pace, location, gives his all
To make each game the best he's ever thrown.
The hitter, like the reader, sees the curve
So teasing, tempting — just outside the plate.
He starts to lunge, then summons up the nerve
To check his swing, and merely watch and wait.
Each poem's a baseball game — each word a pitch
Served up with all its author's special skill.
Each reader's like a fan, who's found his niche
In words and games that never cease to thrill.
With every line and every pitch, it seems
That poets, just like pitchers, offer dreams.

Old Man Parker's Vacant Lot

"Eagle Eyes" they called me
for always finding foul balls
far back of third base in the weeds
of Old Man Parker's vacant lot,
braving shouts of the old man
who craned his turtle neck
toward us from a kitchen window.

"Eagle Eyes" they called me,
but it was more than eyes:
we had only the one ball,
and Old Man Parker would be out
soon to water down his weeds.
Many a day we saw him sitting alone,
watching his precious weeds grow.

Hero

*(Written in the early morning hours of August 26, 1976,
during the last four innings of a game won by the New
York Yankees, 5–4)*

I force my ears open at the bedside radio past midnight,
five hours before dawn, before my rising
to the drudgery of work,
and I hear the Twins–Yankees baseball game
falling into the sixteenth inning and counting.
I owe it to them, playing their hearts out for me,
making pinpoint pitches,
managerial wheels turning like a runaway stagecoach
in some late movie pre-empted on a far off tv screen
where advertisers run out of fresh commercials
and announcers hope for an error,
home run, wild pitch, anything to send them sleepily
toward the airport and a tired trip home.

I pull out gray hairs on my chest one by one
to stay awake and cheer Dick Tidrow,
nine scoreless innings in relief and still going
with an arm that will not comb his hair tomorrow.
Too many would-be heroes spin in wild swings
to break the tie, but arms long ago turned to rubber,
and the ball fluffs off the bat like a shuttlecock,
slowing into its fall far from the inviting sight
of game-ending fences where fans give up regretfully,
forcing the driver of a chartered bus
to transport their group back to the hotel
so a tour guide won't have to wait at eight next morning
for the trip to the UN Building
where action lacks Yankee Stadium's drama.

My hairs grow thin and my chest grows sore
as still another double play sends a new inning
pushing my eyelids down like a shade
over the Yankee Stadium lights,
blacking out the dramatics still to come.
A base hit in the eighteenth snaps me awake
to hear Tidrow leave amid cheers, a hero without a victory
who must depend on someone else's arm
to keep him from defeat. I gain my second wind,
feeling the exhilaration of a marathon man,
hearing a history-making game,
the eleventh longest in Yankee history
with no end in sight.

I begin to fantasize: maybe the game will last until dawn
and by mutual consent the teams will take time out
for breakfast and return to start fresh.
I wonder what fielders will be bothered
by the nine a.m. sun peeking over the stadium roof.
I return to reality in the nineteenth inning,
sensing a Yankee triumph; my aching chest is hairless.
Piniella pinch-hits, fresh arms;
a hit will end the game and send me to the bathroom
where I haven't gone for fear of missing something.

Piniella grounds out weakly.
I sag like a balloon full of water
while my bladder screams for someone to save me.
I know I must act now. I climb out of bed,
and at the instant my foot hits the floor
Mickey Rivers drives the ball
over the center fielder's head.
The Yankees win!
I stare down at my magical foot.
It was all so easy.
Why, I wonder, didn't I get up sooner?

Artificial Baseball

Late summer in its sun-drenched dance of green
Stood watch outside the massive sterile dome
Where air-conditioned artificial turf
Took weary time-warped players far from home.

Past summers, in their breeze-filled victories,
Lit up the parks where players learned to read
The speed of sky, twist of cloud, slant of sun —
The language that they knew they all would need.

Now summer, in its sun-spun loneliness,
Hopes the dome will break, fears it never will.
It senses that the greatest summer game
Lies frozen in the dome's unnatural chill.

Ballplayer

Sorting through his son's belongings,
he found the baseball, souvenir
from a high school no-hitter.
He rolled the ball in his hands,
then gripped it across the seams,
remembering the sharp break
of the curve ball he taught his son,
smiled at his memory of the surprise
on faces of left-handed sluggers
whose swings caught only air.
The ball trembled in his knobby fingers.
He put it back, carefully, in the box.
He dared not risk dropping it,
nor did he want it moistened by tears.

Church League Softball
for the "Over Forties"

Old men.
Once we could run
without our stomachs
crashing against the rib cage,
without our hearts signaling "truce."

Old men.
Once we could backhand
the hardest shots
and, offbalance, throw out speed
from the grass behind short.

Old men.
We are kids again
for seven innings,
playing by memory, not talent;
risking injury, pretending we're not

Old men.
No other game so
alive can be
the fountain of youth for
us otherwise tired, old men.

Center Field Grasses

Beneath my feet on center field grasses
where once I roamed free,
and with abandon
slid on a hard belly of youth
to catch line drives,
now cattle munch,
unaware of history.

Beyond the knee high weeds
I see what was once infield,
hear voices drifting out to me,
like vapor from a bottle,
spanning twenty-five years of absence,
Siren-like voices singing for my return
to those past glories;
I feel myself slipping, slipping,
and wish with slumped shoulders
for something to tie myself to.

There is no rope in the pasture,
only rusty barbed wire.
Torn between the pain of staying
and the futility of going back,
I scan the ground for wax
to plug my ears,
see only dried manure
where once I raced on winged feet
over a smooth cushion of grass.

I look up, wonder if my teenage sons
heard the voices. I guess not;
they sit laughing in the car.
Their eyes had raised silently
in amused wonder
when I stopped here at this old pasture
at the edge of my old home town.
They had never seen this place
when it was not pasture.

They cannot believe that this
balding
heavy
middle-aged man
whose breath comes in
pants climbing a flight
of stairs
was once young, was once a hero
of sorts.

They will not believe that this body
made acrobatic catches, stole bases,
hit home runs, slid head first across
home to beat River Grove and was mobbed
by teammates, carried on their shoulders.

They will not believe that I wanted
more than what I have. They do not know
that compromises must be made.

They do not think that twenty-five years
from now THEY will reminisce
at a long deserted bandstand
while my grandchildren sit amused
unwilling to believe that THEIR FATHER
once played a guitar before ten thousand
pot-smoking, half-dressed, long-haired...

A car horn blasts.
Shouts.
Urges.
Impatient.
My sons are waving for me to hurry up.

I let them honk.
I turn my back to them,
fighting tears,
cursing silently,
wishing I could go back
to voices from long ago,
because my sons are in a hurry:
they don't know who I am.

35

Winner

what I remember most
is my dad behind the rusted screen
back of home plate
"You can hit this guy!"
his voice not letting up
through four fast balls
(two misses swinging late,
two fouls on checked swings)

then the curve ball and the dying quail
into left-center,
the winning run sliding home,
my dad all smiles,
slapping backs in the bleachers
as if HIS single had won the game

No Hit Pitcher, Staying Loose

Between innings,
he alone
jokes in dugouts
stone-
deaf from age-
old superstitions—

three outs
to go, then
time enough
for slapping backs,
to cheer and yell,
if all goes well.

teammates struggle
to ignore
the obvious,
as if their shouts
or their wisecracks
might break the spell—

The Summer That Dreams Forgot

Maybe the players didn't really strike;
maybe I was a minor league Rip Van Winkle
sleeping my way through summer,
sweating my way through a terrible nightmare.

Maybe baseball is still the National Pastime,
loved by devotees not for its oversized chickens
who bait umpires, kiss ballgirls, and tackle players,
but for crack of bat, the magic glove, the slow change.

Maybe the game still lives somewhere, waiting to awaken
us to a reincarnation of the days of Enos and Yogi,
of Stan the Man and the Splendid Splinter and Say Hey
what do you say Willie Mays, of Ford, the Mick, and Sandy.

Maybe the day will come when fielders will stab again
for liners and one-hoppers instead of fat contracts that
lull some into a complacency that catches even the quickest
napping like a third baseman deep on a swinging bunt.

Maybe dreams will live again instead of nightmares,
and newspapers will record averages, not salaries.
Maybe we will never have to approach a dope-smoking
hero and sigh, "Say it ain't so. Say it ain't so."

Snow Baseball

January's the hardest month —
too late for Christmas,
too early for "real" baseball.
We need a game to stop the craving.
There where snow covers the field
like a tarp of frozen cotton,
it's soft enough for sliding
beneath the fluff of flung snowballs,
weak imitations of bullet throws to first
by cold-armed third basemen.
The runner on first breaks as the hitter
signals the hit and run, throws a snowball
toward short, high as a Larry Bowa popup.
He slips and sloshes while the winter ball
shatters against a fielder's mittened hands.
He dives headfirst across a guess of third,
his face kicking up some dust of snow.
He bounces up,
warmed by the kind of thoughts
that help get us through January,
the hardest month.

With the Game on the Line

Last of the ninth, and the ball
spinning its way toward sunlight,
reaching its arc and heading down
to me, shading my eyes with my mitt
for the game is on the line
and I have no place to hide.

Thirteen Ways
of Looking at a Baseball Game

1

home runs,
in batting practice, especially,
when twenty kids maul each other
in the cheap seats for a scuffed ball
they wouldn't give a nickle for
on the playground yesterday, or tomorrow

2

the National Anthem—
sneaking looks at fidgeting players,
trying to find some who,
after a hundred games a year,
still honor the flag, waving stiff toward center,
while they wait for the moment near the end
when the crowd's roar
drowns out the final line

3

the third strike, swinging,
the ball circling the bases,
tying the catcher and infielders together
like a long rope,
while the batting helmet
skips toward the dugout steps like a stone

4

the bleachers,
shirt off, sipping beer, crunching peanuts,
cheering like at a college football game,
tossing dimes to the left fielder
after good hustle on a smash to the wall,
almost forgetting that Monday
takes me back inside from nine to five
and snapping at my wife after work
just because she's there

5

the free agent,
last year's favorite player;
me insisting all winter
that he was not to blame
for selling out to the enemy,
finally rationalizing that his replacement,
hitting .240 now, but a gamer,
has far better tools anyhow

6

the umpire's half pivot
toward first base,
reaching out for his strike call
as if wishing to pull it back,
then turning in slow motion
toward the mound, crouching,
resting his hands on the catcher's shoulders
like a father teaching his son to stay low

7

the expert, rednecked in front of me,
bleating to his wife all he knows,
that the league's top hitter chokes
with runners in scoring position,
has a throwing arm erratic
as a rookie southpaw pitcher,
makes too much money to be motivated;
that same hitter's two-run double quiets him,
but not the wife, who says,
"Really? Which team is he on?"

8

the catcher,
five feet down the third base line,
low like a defensive lineman
in a goal line stand;
he takes the ball and the hard-flying shoulder
together,
exploding across the plate,
lying dazed even after the crowd's roar
tells him he held the ball

9

the shift —
the field tilts to the left;
infielders slide toward third
from the weight of the slugger
swinging right handed
toward walls as inviting
as prom kisses,
ignoring the vast emptiness of right field
which offers him nothing
but the cold touch of a single

10

the reliever
stalking in from the pen,
all business,
snatches the ball, lets fly —
he flat out doesn't care
the bags are loaded
for the top rbi man
and a single will win it —
he flat out plans to fan the turkey

11

the vendor
bellowing "COLD BEER HERE,"
seemingly unaware
of the magical tenth inning game situation
when all but the shallowest of fans
are standing as one
in that fragile, timeless moment
between beers

12

the losers,
shuffling toward the locker room,
head-bowed-glum or dirt-kicking-mad,
ignoring catcalls from frustrated fans,
as even the best of them must
at least sixty or seventy times a season,
living for tomorrow, when the first pitch
spinning toward the plate erases all the past,
when even the worst have equal hopes of heroics

13

the stadium,
almost empty now
except for the last of fans drifting out,
the ground crew readying for another day,
a lone player near the dugout with a group of four;
the crunch of peanut shells beneath my feet,
the line of sun climbing the right field wall,
my bent scorecard penciled full of memories
for those freezing winter nights
waiting for spring

Watching the Montgomery Rebels
Play Baseball at Patterson Field

I wish we could—my sons, my wife, me.
Illinois natives, longtime neighbors
of Wrigley Field and Comisky Park,
we planned our move to Montgomery,
searching in THE SPORTING NEWS
for new teams to watch. We read of
(sang praises to) the Double A Rebels.

In off-season, 1980, we arrived
and scouted Patterson Field,
peering through cracks and holes
toward next summer's baseball.
We dreamed of doubles crushing plank fences,
of home runs sinking into ivy-clung hills
overlooking the field.

We prepared our throats to cheer
hungry Rebel heroes, two years
(or forever) away from stardom.
The Rebels moved that winter,
giving Birmingham the best of future summers,
leaving behind Rebel ghosts. They float
above second base as I drive by at twilight.

I point to them, but my wife does not see.
Through the open window I hear the ghosts whisper
as they face the paint-chipped bleachers
empty behind home plate.
The half-formed phrases echo in my head:
"Too late... Too late..."
My wife turns to me on the front seat.
"Too late for what?" she asks.

Throwing Rainbows from Deep Short

"Could I hit? Well, look at this,"
I tell my sons, whipping open
my high school yearbook,
to black-inked proof on page 71:

	AB	H	BA.
Gene Fehler	48	21	.437

No need to say that I hit only
nine balls to the outfield,
five of them bat-handle bloopers
dying in no-man's land in short right.

No need to say that only my good speed
saved my average,
getting me eight bunt singles.

No need to say that most of my
other safeties came on slow ground balls
to weak-armed shortstops, whose rainbow throws
floated like parachutes to first base
after my foot had already found
the precious bag, that pot of gold
that buys my middle-aged glory.

Left-Handed Poetry

this is a left-handed poem,
written in the midnight pain
of a broken collarbone,
my poetry arm

the pen feels strange
in my left hand; no wonder
Koufax had control problems
for awhile

in time
perhaps I will write
a left-handed
Hall of Fame poem

but now,
words jump around on the page
like rising fast balls
out of the strike zone

this is a left-handed poem,
and I've been sent
to the minor leagues
to develop finesse,

a change of pace,
to prove myself
all over again
to those fickle fans

who have already forgotten
that my right-handed poems
were nothing less
than overpowering

First Time at Bat

Chalk-scarred on-deck circle
spotlights the boy
trying to hide under the glare of eyes.
With arms thin as link sausage
he swings two bats to check the speed
of warm-up tosses
while the pitcher's mammoth shadow
darkens the third base line.

Lips tight, he steps in,
eyes the winding pitcher,
too embarrased to peek toward
where the proud bleacher voice booms,
"You can do it, son."
The boy prays not for the miracle
that he might hit the ball,
simply for the comfort of a good excuse.

Belated Thanks to "Bud" Bull,
My First Baseball Coach

Tony Gwynn's short bat brought thoughts of you,
of your bold coaching strategy
that day when I was thirteen,
bursting with pride over the new bat
I'd bought myself with money
earned mowing lawns, pulling weeds.

Thirty-six inches of bat,
long enough to stack dozens
of home runs in its thick barrel.
and me barely five feet tall.
I choked so high the knob punched
my stomach on each choppy swing.

"Let me try it," you said,
signaling for the pitcher's smoke.
Your strength matched your name.
Pitch after pitch caught the fat part;
man-sized home runs flew out,
but you did not smile.

Then that final pitch,
the handle splitting like firewood.
"Sorry," you said. "I'll buy you another."
And you did.
Thirty-one inches. Child's bat.
When I choked up, the knob missed my stomach.

Christmas Eve, 1957

July's sun sweeps the green top
of Louie's basement ping pong table.
Its glare erases the swoosh of wind
swirling snow against the windows.
APBA Baseball.
Yankees 3, Indians 2 —
one on, two out,
bottom of 12th.
Then the final roll:

The large die shouts "6";
The small die slaps a cardboard box.
Spins.
Their breathing stops until it
spins itself into a little "6."
Louie explodes with laughter, relief.
They watch Vic Wertz circle the bases
behind former bat champ Bobby Avila.
Teddy's Yanks have lost a heart-breaker.

After they tabulate statistics,
Teddy trudges home through dark snow,
wistfully glancing toward the sky,
ears attuned to lost sleighbells.
He hopes his mom will be back from her date
and that she will have lit the Christmas tree
behind their iced living room window,
a tiny last-minute reminder
of how Christmas used to be.

Ever Reaching

Across a thousand miles
and thirty years
pink wisps of evening clouds
caught high fly balls
we hit there,
then threw them back
toward our outstretched hands.
I thought we had caught them all,
but this evening
the wisps of clouds have returned.

I didn't search them out;
they followed ME as if to tell
of something I'd forgotten.
I watch to see some long-lost
baseball drop from a pink heaven
toward these clumsy hands
which have almost forgotten
the gifts to be received
from the simple act
of stretching ever upward.

Wordsworth Never Lost at Baseball

"Emotion recollected in
tranquility,"
Wordsworth said, he

who never saw a grand slam
in the ninth
steal certain victory.

He can recollect all he wants
of Michael,
of Lucy beside the springs of Dove,

of London's stagnant waters,
of the world
laying waste its powers.

But what's he know of pain:
he
who never lost at baseball.

Graveyard

Our baseball diamond has vanished,
turned into a kiddy playground
no different from a million others.
I prefer seeing it as it was:
just behind third base, twenty feet or so,
railroad tracks cut toward left-center,
slicing part of our outfield away.

Any ball over the tracks was out,
but the ditch (three feet deep,
three feet across) that paralleled the tracks,
was in play. So were three skinny birches
back of second base.
We knew the field blindfolded those summer days
before Little League parks grew in boring symmetry.

We knew how to place hits
away from the tracks,
knew how to drop pop flies
that stopped inches short of railway ties,
knew how to time leaps across ditches
in acrobatic wonder
to spear fly balls.

The field's gone now, long gone.
Swings, slides, jungle gyms
entertain children too young for a Little League
which waits for them with schedules,
umpires, frantic parents and real fences
all in absolute
symmetry.

He Might Even Win

i might miss
for the first time
my son's baseball game,
tonight,
at Leland
too far to walk
and my van broken down.

he needs me there
i tell myself;
he needs my cheering,
my support;
but the game will go on
without me
(they might even win).

so will the world go on
when i am gone;
my son will play
the game of life
without my cheers,
my support,
and he might even win.

Bubby's Error

It's still clear in my mind: that Sunday afternoon
when I was eight, Bubby in his prime on a bumpy infield
in the middle of what was little more than cow pasture.
 "Keep your eyes on Bubby!" my father would urge
 every inning when our side took the field.
 "Watch Bubby, he's the best there is!"
And in the ninth, based loaded—a grounder right at him.
We would win by one. Except the ball skipped
off his glove. Into short left. Two runners scored.
 Everyone except Bubby left the field, our team with heads down,
 opponents shouting and cheering. My father didn't say a word,
 just grabbed my arm and half pulled me to our car.
I glanced back and saw Bubby alone on the field. He stood
still as a painting for a moment, hands on his hips, staring
straight ahead. Then, in a smooth, continuous flow,
 he fielded a phantom grounder, made a phantom toss
 to second. It was effortless, almost in slow motion.
 Then he stood, hands on his hips once again.
A moment later he reached down, picked up
a couple of pebbles, flipped them on the outfield grass.
By now we were at our car and I couldn't see anymore.
 "We shoulda won it" is all I remember my father saying
 all the way home, gunning that Packard way up to 55.
 Muttering, like a broken record, "We shoulda won it."
In the years that followed I saw Bubby field a thousand
grounders, but the image that never leaves me is that
Sunday when I was eight, him with his hands on his hips,
 then sweeping into that phantom scoop, that phantom toss
 to second, the flip of pebbles into the outfield grass.
 So when my own kids were old enough for baseball,
I took them to games, (except it was softball now) and
Bubby, heavier, was over at first, handling throws
from younger, quicker guys, showing them how to win.
 And what I told my sons over and over, at least
 until they were old enough to judge for themselves,
 was: "Watch Bubby! He's the best there is!"

Ever Young

He's one of those guys
who thinks he is younger
than he is.

You know the type:
playing softball two nights a week,
huffing and puffing around the bases,
believing he can run fast as ever,
not realizing that the only reason
the ball fell in for a hit
is because the defense
is fat and slow itself.

His heart attack has slowed him down
for awhile,
but it won't slow him down for long.

Bet on it.

He's one of those guys
who'll die before he gets old —
or live trying.

Coach Chose Me

After a day at the beach
when the sun's sting
paled in importance to the sight of skin
still virgin white at fleshed edges
of just-right bikinis,
Coach chose me.

I didn't volunteer.
Not with my legs boiled-lobster pink.
With every step my legs rubbed raw against my jeans,
more painful even than being ignored
by a lakeful of teenage lovelies.
But, unaware that the rest of me
matched my vermillion face,
not seeing my agony,
Coach chose me.

"Today we'll learn the right way to slide."
Coach slapped his huge hand on my shoulder,
which shouted red thoughts
beneath the t-shirt I'd put on too late.
"Gene will demonstrate."
It made perfect sense. Me,
the team's fastest baserunner,
its best base-stealer,
a master of every kind of slide, so
Coach chose me.

I slid perfectly, time after time,
with the left leg, right leg,
hooking the bag just so,
better than anyone, while all the while
fire shot through my jeans,
but I did not cry out.
I suffered in proud silence
because I knew I deserved it all:
the agony and the glory
of that long-ago evening when
Coach chose me.

The Day the Bear Died

We hit grounders, pop-ups,
line drives, fly balls for hours,
Curtis and me those high-school
summer days
dreaming of the big leagues.
"Can't waste a minute," we said,
growing greater day-by-day
while little Joey
from across the street adored his heroes,
Curtis and me,
who could catch balls hit into the clouds,
stop liners like Superman catching bullets.

We honored him sometimes
with a word or smile,
basking in glory
until that day in the dead heat of August
when three sixth graders,
for a laugh,
ripped from tiny hands Joey's teddy,
tore off the legs and arms,
slashed the body with their jackknives.

I back-handed a one-hopper,
accepting praise from Curtis,
ignoring
Joey's futile screams:
I was on my way to being great.

Immortals

My sons both played this week,
unsuspecting models for my telephoto.
One son pitched a shutout, winning
the championship for his team.
The other played the last inning
in a lost cause and struck out.
Amid color prints of the cat
and garden and tree house,
my sons will pitch and bat.
Immortals, both.
Forever equal in the magnified eye.

Veteran Ballplayer

Season after season
the steady downpour of age
washes over me.
It wears me down,
carries me in a torrent
toward the ultimate rainout.
Dark clouds hover above me.
I dimly remember sunlight,
days of outfield grass
dry and quick
beneath my feet.
Each night I switch channels
to a new weatherman,
hoping to find one
with a forecast forever free
from the threat of rain.

Deathbed Showdown

Death goes into its stretch,
uncoils toward the wasted body
lying on hospital sheets like a dried leaf.
The dying man sees the pitch coming,
grips his son's hand.
Then, his voice a cracked whisper,
takes his best swing:
"Remember . . . the game against Westfield,
you were twelve . . . maybe thirteen . . .
your double . . . with two out
in the last inning . . . won it.
You came through, son! You came through."
The son squeezes his father's hand,
knows the end is imminent,
knows, too, that in his father's final moments
something has outdueled Death.

Part Two:
Parodies from the Classics

Each of the poems in this section imitates the form or rhythm and rhyme of a "classic" poem. The poem and poet that provided the model for each of the parodies are identified immediately after each poem.

To Bunt, or Not to Bunt

To bunt, or not to bunt, — that is the question: —
Whether 'tis safer in the end to challenge
The arm of a hard-charging third baseman
Or to try slashing a line drive past him,
And in the process end him? — To hit, — to swing
Once more; and by a swing we try to end
The heartache of a botched-up bunt attempt
That ends the rally, — 'tis all too commonplace
And is not to be wished. To hit, — to swing;
To swing! perchance to bounce one off the rug,
For off that AstroTurf what bounce may fly
Above the reach of fielders' leaping stabs
Must make us gasp: there's the surprise
That brings a fine excitement to this game.
Those bounces do make heroes of us all,
And thus the happy choice to swing away
Makes sickly by contrast the thought to bunt;
And pennant races often are determined
By this small choice; and history changes.
And now's the time for action. — Soft you now!
The sign is flashed to me. — Coach, in thy signals
Be all my skills remembered.

(William Shakespeare: "To Be, or Not to Be" from Hamlet*)*

But I Was One-and-Twenty

When I was one-and-twenty
    I heard a wise coach say,
"Swing hard, and do it daily —
    A thousand swings a day;
And hit behind the runner
    Till it comes naturally."
But I was one-and-twenty,
    No use to talk to me.

When I was one-and-twenty
    I heard him tell me this,
"You try to pull all pitches,
    And that is why you miss."
Advice? He gave me plenty;
    I ignored his fine critique.
Now I am two-and-twenty,
    And got released last week.

(A.E. Housman: "When I Was One-and-Twenty")

The Cubbies of Chicago

Success is counted sweetest
By those who ne'er succeed.
The Cubbies of Chicago—
A classic case indeed.

Not one of Stengel's champions
Who earned World Series pay
Could know the satisfaction
Cub fans will feel someday

When—if by a miracle—
The Cubs should finally win;
The Bleacher Bums will deafen
Chicago with their din.

(Emily Dickinson: "Success Is Counted Sweetest")

A Red-Faced Father

so much depends
upon

a red-faced
father

gazing from gray
bleachers

behind his son's
dugout

(William Carlos Williams: "A Red Wheelbarrow")

The Cub Star

Once on Wrigley Field bleachers while I sat with saddened features
Pondering the fate of Cubbies who made mental errors galore,
Suddenly I saw a rookie playing third, a smooth, smooth cookie,
Just as smooth as any rookie I had ever seen before.
"He will stumble soon," I muttered, "as Cubs often have before.
    I can't let my spirits soar."

Ah, the annual aggravation as our springtime jubilation
Turned to sorrow as the losses were too numerous to ignore.
Glad I was I had found someone who could throw and hit and run—
An absolute phenomenon—who'd easily go three for four,
Turn double plays and bunt and be a player I could adore
    On the Cubs forevermore.

And the way he ran the bases brought new life to all our faces
For he filled us with excitement hardly ever felt before.
He would be our team's salvation from our longtime tribulation
Buried, as we were, somewhere beneath the cold, dark cellar floor.
He would lead us from the depths till we could all with triumph roar:
    "Respectability—once more!"

Suddenly our hearts were broken when those awful words were spoken:
"Filing for free agency"—our favorite Cub, the very core
Of the team he'd make contenders—yet still close to tail-enders,
Oh, those dreadful Cub pretenders—trying to escape the floor,
Where we'd be if we were victims of that great free agent war
    As we often were before.

"Stay, please stay," we fans all shouted, even though we really doubted
That a player of his worth would stay a single season more.
Now the opposition's stronger, and Cub fans will sorrow longer
And the current Cubbies roster we'll continue to deplore.
Just as long as talent's taken by that great free agent war,
    We shall sorrow—evermore.

(Edgar Allan Poe: "The Raven")

Note: This poem was written with Ryne Sandberg in mind. Fortunately, Sandberg stayed with the Cubs, moved to second base, and helped restore the Cubs to respectability.

Ebbets Field

Don't tear the treasured ballpark down!
    Long has it brought me joy,
As many a Brooklyn player has
    That I've watched as a boy.
Above it rings Red Barber's voice
    Amidst the crowd's deep roar—
The summer sounds that would be heard
    By Brooklyn fans no more.

Her fences, dented by those balls
    That Gil and Campy hit;
Pete Reiser's battles with the walls—
    No, he did not submit.
No more would Carl and Snider speed
    Across the outfield grass
Nor Reese and Jackie take the lead
    In demonstrating class.

Oh, let the mighty field stand
    As tribute to her past.
The loyalty of all her fans
    Can never be surpassed.
Forget the California gold;
    Let loyalty prevail,
For loyalty of Brooklyn fans
    Can never be for sale!

(Oliver Wendell Holmes: "Old Ironsides")

In Late —

in Late-
fall when the earth is just-
frozen the echo
of basehits

rattles here and there

but keithandbilly go
yapping through football and
basketball and it's
winter

when my mind is stir-crazy

the memory
of basehits rattles
here and there
and tonyandjoe wait beyond

the ice-storms and winter-sports until

it's
spring
when
        the
                ever-present
baseHits rattle
here
and
there

(E.E. Cummings: "In Just — ")

Note: Keith Jackson and Billy Packer were announcing college football and basketball games, respectively, and Tony Kubek and Joe Garagiola were announcing baseball games.

The Ball Leaps Up

The ball leaps up from sun-baked clay
    In hot Atlanta's park.
So was it when July began
And stays while flames of summer fan.
The field's like a frying pan.
    Too hot to play.
If nothing else, I sport a tan.
And yet I wish my games could be
Played under domes, artificially.

(William Wordsworth: "My Heart Leaps Up")

Note: Certain Atlanta Braves infielders have been known to blame their errors on the hard ground in Atlanta's Fulton County Stadium.

I Marvel at the Ways of Ryne

I marvel at the ways of Ryne
    For time and time again
I see him play above the heads
    Of lesser, mortal, men.

(E.B. White: "I Marvel at the Ways of God")

I Have a Rendezvous This Fall

I have a rendezvous this fall
On some World Series battleground
Where I will gladly take the mound
To pitch my team to victory—
I have a rendezvous this fall
And that is where I long to be.

It may be I shall pitch a game
Which brings me life's undying fame
And I shall be revered by all—
It may be my most glorious day.
I have a rendezvous this fall
On some World Series holiday
Where strong opponents take their place
To try to drive me to disgrace.

God knows that nervousness will creep
Into my heart as cameras' eyes
Peer in close-up, pan and sweep
Across me as I hurl the ball;
They might see fear upon my face...
But I've a rendezvous this fall
To capture baseball's grandest prize
And start to take my rightful place
As one of baseball's honored few,
And I'll not fail that rendezvous.

(Alan Seeger: "I Have a Rendezvous with Death")

The Charge of the Mighty Wade

Major league, major league,
Major league phenom.
All of us watched as Wade Boggs
    Climbed toward four hundred.
    "Slug all those line drives, Wade!
Hit that ball hard!" we said.
All of us watched as Wade Bogs
    Climbed toward four hundred.
        "Slug all those line drives, Wade!"
        Was Rod Carew dismayed
        As his own average dipped
            Far under four hundred?
        He might have made a sigh,
        Perhaps even wondered why
        His own average had to die
        As we all watched Wade Boggs
        Climb toward four hundred.
Line drives to right of them,
Line drives to left of them,
Line drives far over them
    Rattled and thundered;
Wade stood there straight and tall
And blasted every ball
Out of the fielders' grasp.
As the season moved on, we all
    Knew he'd reach four hundred.
        Slapped doubles here and there,
        Slapped singles everywhere,
        Boggs on a batting tear,
        Raising his average, while
        All of us wondered:
        Two more tough months remained;
        Could enough points be gained?
        Carew and George Brett
        Reeled from the summer heat,
            Faltered and stumbled.
        Their average dropped, but Boggs
        Climbed toward four hundred.

Line drives to right of them,
Line drives to left of them,
Line drives far over them
    Rattled and thundered.
Wade stood there straight and tall.
Even if he should fall
Short of that goal we'd all
Hoped the great Boggs could reach,
He'd tried his best to be
First since Ted Williams
    To hit four hundred.
        When will his glory fade?
        O the wild charge of Wade!
          All the world wondered.
        Honor the charge he made!
        Honor the mighty Wade!
          On toward four hundred!

(Alfred Lord Tennyson: "The Charge of the Light Brigade")

Note: This was written late in the 1983 season, when Boggs' average climbed steadily and while George Brett's and Rod Carew's averages tumbled.

An Over-the-Hill Pinch-Hitter

From my dugout sleep I trudge up to the plate
And I doze in my crouch till the pitcher throws.
Sixty feet away, loosed like a deadly knife,
Come the high hard ones and the nightmare sliders.
When I whiff they'll wash me out of the league, I suppose.

(Randall Jarrell: "The Death of the Ball Turret Gunner")

To Jose Canseco

It's fun to dream
(I often do)
That I both look
And play like you.

I sprint. I crush
A home run ball.
I do these things
In dreams, that's all.

(Richard Armour: "To a Human Skeleton")

A Certain Slant of Curve

There's a certain slant of curve,
On summer afternoons,
That confounds me, which is why
Our manager platoons.

A mortal hurt it gives me —
Baseball's greatest scar:
The biggest difference
'Tween substitute and star.

Baseball offers me a chance
To be a millionaire,
But when that curve comes breaking,
I haven't got a prayer.

When it comes, the catcher listens
For the words, "You're out!"
That awful certain slant of curve
Is what this game's about.

(Emily Dickinson: "A Certain Slant of Light")

71

Casey and the Dome

The sunshine wasn't brilliant on the Mudville nine that day
Because a new domed stadium now covered them at play.
So when opposing batters hit the ball an awesome height,
No globe of nasty sun glared down to blind young Casey's sight.

Some fans and players argued that the dome had changed the game,
Had tampered with tradition. But young Casey saw no blame.
He believed that playing baseball on a rug indoors was keen.
His feet stayed dry, his body cool. His uniform stayed clean.

"Oh, what a treat!" young Casey said. "This game is now a breeze.
It used to be we'd roast in June, and in October, freeze.
It used to be the wind would gust and take a routine fly
And push it far beyond the fence; 'twould make a pitcher cry.

"Too often in the past," said Casey, "fly balls hit the sun
And sailed far beyond my grasp and cost our team a run.
No longer do I have to work to shade my blinded eyes.
Whoever thought of domes to play in certainly was wise."

The comforts that the dome provided all seemed pretty nice,
Like keeping dry in thunderstorms. Why, that was paradise.
For Casey, as a boy, had caused his mother great distress
While playing baseball in the rain and coming home a mess.

So even now the thought of muddy uniforms was grim.
To play inside and not get wet made perfect sense to him.
When Casey heard his teammates growl, "This indoor stuff's absurd,"
He paid them no attention, like he hadn't even heard.

The oldtime fans, the stubborn ones, just didn't seem to know
That domes were here to stay, and parks like Fenway had to go.
And in Chicago's Wrigley Field, the ivy soon would die
The moment that a shiny dome could block it from the sky.

So Casey played beneath the dome a year — then two — then three,
Ignoring (trying to, at least) his chronic painful knee.
The artificial turf, it's said, had caused his knee to hurt.
"So what?" young Casey said. "It still beats playing in the dirt."

The crowds that watched young Casey play were noted for their noise;
They claimed their shouts made opposition players lose their poise.
Yet soon ear-splitting screams reverberating from the crowd
Seemed whispers to his failing ears, no longer even loud.

A fourth year came, a fifth — the dome began to lose its charm,
And Casey realized the dome brought much less good than harm.
The ball bounced true, yet often bounced above his frantic leap;
High bounding homers now were what made Casey's pitchers weep.

The sun, 'tis true, was not a factor in the domelit sky;
And yet, too often, Casey lost a routine-looking fly
That soared up toward the painted dome, into the roof of white;
The ball, the dome, were all as one to Casey's failing sight.

The dome destroyed poor Casey. His potential — unfulfilled.
No longer was he cheered by fans, those fans who once he thrilled
With his exuberance, his joy, devotion to the game.
Five years of indoor play had made him disillusioned, lame.

Oh, in those outdoor stadiums, the sun shines warm and bright.
A breeze wafts gently o'er the fields, and players' hearts are light.
But somewhere in this modern world, outside a dismal dome,
A mother waits as Casey, deaf yet clean, limps sadly home.

(Ernest Thayer: "Casey at the Bat")

73

If God Were a Baseball Pitcher

I honestly don't think it nice
To end the world in fire or ice.
I think a better way to go
Would be for God to take His stretch,
Then glance toward Hell and turn and throw
So hard that no one there could catch
This ball we're on, this crazy sphere,
And we'd end up quite far from here,
Perhaps somewhere in Paradise.

(Robert Frost: "Fire and Ice")

Believe Me, If All Those Enduring Old Arms

Believe me, if all those enduring old arms,
    Which I gaze on so fondly today,
Lost their masterful pitches which still work like charms,
    They could still put great hitters away.
For great hurlers like those pitch with both head and heart:
    They have more than just physical skill:
A strong arm is nice, but one needs to be smart
    To have lasting success on the hill.

There will always be young men who try to dethrone
    The old-timers we've grown to revere,
Who ignore ages' aches and find ways to postpone
    That last day of a lengthy career.
When the end finally comes, may there be no regrets,
    For all things have to pass, I suppose.
May careers end like days, with a brilliance that lets
    Us all witness a beautiful close.

(Thomas Moore: "If All Those Endearing Old Charms")

Larrupin' Lou Gehrig

Larrupin' Lou, he did not mourn,
    Successful over many seasons.
He rejoiced that he was born,
    And he had reasons.

Larrupin' was a sight to behold;
    He helped the Yankees go on winning.
His character: it was extolled,
    While Babe was sinning.

Larrupin' earned all that he got;
    He seldom rested from his labor.
And through the years he made a lot
    Of pitchers quaver.

Larrupin' loved his work and wife,
    Combining power, poise, and grace.
He gave all he had to life
    Without disgrace.

Lou must have known what lay ahead
    When he spoke of hope, and fans all cried:
"I am the luckiest man..." he said.
    Too soon, he died.

(Edwin Arlington Robinson: "Miniver Cheevy")

Here's to the All-Star

Here's to the All-Star who hits three fifteen;
    Here's to the sub at one fifty;
Here's to the fastest baserunner we've seen,
    And here's to the one who's no swifty.
        Let the toast pass,
        Drink one more glass
To the sport that no other sport can surpass.

Here's to the sluggers whose homers we prize,
    Now to the one who's hit none, sir;
Here's to those hurlers with fast balls that rise,
    And here's to those who all lack one, sir.
        Let the toast pass,
        Drink one more glass
To the sport that no other sport can surpass.

Here's to the shortstop who moves and can throw;
    Now to him who is quite stationary;
Here's to the man who's a consummate pro,
    And now to the man who's not very.
        Let the toast pass,
        Drink one more glass
To the sport that no other sport can surpass.

For if they play hungry, with plenty of vim,
    While at bat or while toting the leather;
I'll happily fill my glass up to the brim,
    And drink as we toast them together.
        Let the toast pass,
        Drink one more glass
To the sport that no other sport can surpass.

(Richard Brinsley Sheridan: "Let the Toast Pass")

Knuckleball

The knuckler hops
on little frog legs.

It comes grinning,
jumps as the slugger
swings from his heels,
and then, moves on.

(Carl Sandburg: "Fog")

Adcock Miss'd Me

Adcock miss'd me when he sped
    Toward the mound to get his licks in.
Though he planned to smash my head,
    My dugout saved me; I leapt in.
Say I'm cowardly, or
    Say fame's lips have never kiss'd me;
Yet I lived to pitch again, for
    Adcock miss'd me.

(Leigh Hunt: "Jenny Kiss'd Me")

Note: Legend has it that Milwaukee Braves first baseman Joe Adcock once charged the mound to get at Giants pitcher Ruben Gomez. Gomez wisely did not wait to ask Adcock what he wanted; he sprinted toward his dugout, and safety.

Baseball of You I Sing

"next to of course god america and
apple pie baseball of you i sing oh
musical antics of gas house gang's band
take me out to the ballgame joltin' joe
where have you gone tinker to evers to
chance the house that ruth built hit 'em where they
ain't them bases on balls oh say can you
see and yes there are those who would still play
for love diving for balls lined up before
the game with autographs the shout play ball
they dash from dugouts quick as hunted deer
that seventh world series game in the fall
and what can life offer for an encore?"

He spoke. And waved for another beer

(E.E. Cummings: "next to of course god")

Reflections on a Pitchers' Duel

Scoring's   But pitching's
Not boring   Bewitching!

(Ogden Nash: "Reflections on Ice-Breaking")

Grabbing an Illegal Bat at Yankee Stadium

Whose bat this is I think I know.
It's caked with pine tar high and low.
The Goose is shivering with fear
To think how far the ball might go.

I'll wait until defeat is near
And then I'll suddenly appear
To make those foolish umpires take
Away the win K.C. earned here.

So what if George Brett's heart will break?
The pennant race is still at stake.
And though my tactics might seem cheap,
I'm out to win, make no mistake.

The pine tar's lovely, dark and deep
Enough to make the Royals weep.
This victory is ours to keep,
This victory is ours to keep.

(Robert Frost: "Stopping by Woods on a Snowy Evening")

Note: This might have been what Yankee manager Billy Martin was thinking moments before George Brett hit his two-out, two-run, ninth inning home run against "Goose" Gossage to give the Royals a 4–3 lead at Yankee Stadium. Martin then protested that Brett's bat was illegally coated with pine tar. The umpires agreed and called Brett out, giving the Yankees an apparent victory. League president Lee McPhail later overruled the umpires. Brett's home run was restored, and the Royals later won the completed game.

The Bench-Warmer

If I should whiff, think only this of me:
    That there's some corner of a dugout bench
That is for ever mine. There shall be
    A thirst inside me that I can never quench;
A thirst for stardom, for the Hall of Fame.
    The water cooler sitting at my side
Can't quench that thirst nor glorify my name
    Nor can it make me the least bit satisfied.

And think, this heart, how hope can be restored,
    A hit, or even some hard-ripped line drive
        To help build up my sagging confidence;
Oh, to be a starter, and adored;
    To finally feel the fame for which I strive
        And which can't be achieved on some cold bench.

(Rupert Brooke, "The Soldier")

To My Fans, on Becoming a Free Agent

Tell me not, fans, I am unkind
    For saying my good-bye
And leaving your kind cheers behind
    While I to new fans fly.

True, I have lost your sweet embrace
    While on your rival's field;
But I have viewed the market place
    And seen what it can yield.

Though my disloyalty is such
    That all you fans abhor,
It's not that I don't love you much:
    I just love money more.

(Richard Lovelace, "To Lucasta, Going to the Wars")

80

Baseball's Harmony

I think that I shall never see
A game that could mean more to me.

A game that God I believe has blest,
For it's more glorious than the rest.

A game that folks all ages play —
And most for pleasure, not for pay.

A game of skill beyond compare
On summer sunlit days so fair.

Whose playing fields entertain
With memories that long remain.

No verses penned by folk like me
Can capture baseball's harmony.

(Joyce Kilmer: "Trees")

Song of the Open Base

I wonder if I'll ever see
A pitcher pitch a pitch to me.
Unless my average starts to fall,
I may not see a strike at all.

(Ogden Nash: "Song of the Open Road")

Note: When George Brett's batting average was hovering around .400, Tiger manager Sparky Anderson pitched around him, vowing that he wouldn't let the hot Brett beat him.

The House That Ruth Built

This mighty home of kings, this noble park,
This plot of tradition, this land of Babe,
This rebuilt heaven, only semi-changed,
This three-tiered stadium, cage for all fair balls
Hit by most powerful of mortal men,
This happy place of cheers, this world of joy,
This precious ground where Series games were played
In more Octobers than on other grass,
Where thrilling names of former greats still ring
Above the lesser bells of other stars,
This blessed realm, this field, this Yankee Stadium...

(William Shakespeare: "This Mighty Home of Kings" from Richard II*)*

We Real Insecure

THE BASEBALL MANAGERS.
SEVEN WITH NEW ONE-YEAR CONTRACTS.

We think win. We
Tailspin. We

Bench star. We
Called "czar." We

Also rans. We
Blast fans. We

Still swoon. We
Fired soon.

(Gwendolyn Brooks, "We Real Cool")

Some Keep the Sabbath on the Mound

Some keep the Sabbath going to Church —
I keep it, on the Mound —
With the National Anthem my first Hymn —
And "Play Ball!" a sacred sound —

Some keep the Sabbath playing Golf —
I go to the Park,
Where opponents try hitting my Best Curve Ball —
I pray they miss the Mark.

My arm delivers my best Sermon —
May the sermon be very strong
And the music sung by the Catcher's loud mitt —
Be strike outs, my best song.

(Emily Dickinson: "Some Keep the Sabbath Going to Church")

Out of Luck, Dave Kingman

Dave Kingman stood, uncoiled as he swung,
And sent breezes from the force of his swings;
Long home runs flew far over the fences,
And from where I sat I could almost count
Five division crowns one behind the other
Under the sunset off Lake Michigan.
And Kingman swung with might, swung with might
Each time up, bearing the weight of the team.
And nothing happened: losses followed wins.
Give me more hits, I wish I might have said
To get more consistency from King Kong
Instead of his strike outs with men on base.
Then Kingman, angered at newspapermen,
Told them, "Sorry, I'm through talking to you."
As if they did not know what sorry meant,
They leaped at Kingman, or they seemed to leap,
And threw him to the wolves. From that time on,
Losses multiplied. And the Kong!
His response was to sulk and go fishing,
And he swung wildly at outside curve balls,
And I appealed, trying to mold the team
To a smooth unit. Then I saw it all—
King Kong, trying to carry the whole team
With home runs no one else knew how to hit.
It was not enough. "Get rid of Kingman.
He's not a team player," the newsmen said.
So. But the magic was gone already.
The fans joined in with derisive boos.
Kingman swung with might and struck out more.
And I watched from the dugout and took fright.
I tried not to believe. The team fell apart.
Little—less—nothing! And that ended it.
The thrill from the mighty Kingman home runs
Had stopped, and fickle fans all turned away.

(Robert Frost: "Out, Out—")

*Note: Kingman almost single-handedly carried the Cubs through the 1979 season
and then suffered through a sub-par 1980.*

I Knew a Man Named Stengel

nobody loses all the time

i knew a man named
Stengel who was born eccentric and
nearly nobody said he should have gone
into dentistry perhaps because that man Stengel could
talk Double Talk That Would Make Halloween Sound Like
    Christmas itself which
may or may not account for the fact that the man

Stengel took on that possibly most precarious
profession that is to say if big
league manager might be called
by any stretch of
the imagination
profession

that man Stengel's team
failed because his Brooklyn
pitchers were so cold
the man Stengel saw them
finish toward the bottom
three years straight so when

that man Stengel
had a Boston team his
hitters stank so loud that
six years running
the man Stengel watched them
last in hitting or almost

and at the end with the Mets
he almost drowned in sorrow the man Stengel a victor
not too often as he slept in the
dugout while trying not to watch three hundred forty
defeats as ten pitchers lost seventeen or
more in three years so to speak at the helm

i remembered we shed no tears because
of the man Stengel's nine pennants in
eleven Yankee glory seasons
(and man, especially
the man
Stengel

never loses all the time)   *[E.E. Cummings: "nobody loses all the time"]*

A Noiseless Patient Owner

A noiseless patient owner,
I marked how strange it was that I had never seen one of these
    creatures,
Marked how instead they seemed to be quite blustery.
They launched forth virulence, virulence, virulence, out of
    themselves,
Ever berating players, ever angering the fans.

And you, this great game where you stand
Surrounded, as it were, by those oceans of ego
Ceaselessly screaming, threatening, taking credit for players'
    performance,
Till the players, embittered, play for themselves and no one
    else,
Til the fans, frustrated, turn away from this once great game.

(Walt Whitman: "A Noiseless Patient Spider")

Note: As a life-long Yankee fan trying hard not to let that love die, I found an easy target for this poem.

Baseball Announcers

The sports announcer: critical and windy,
A physical disgrace, though not yet forty,
Never played ball himself, so it is said,
Yet mocks a runner: "He's got legs like lead." —
Is critical of how a pitcher throws,
And hands out batting tips — as if he knows.

(Theodore Roethke, "Pipling")

Don Larsen's Perfect Game

'Twas October, and Don Larsen's throws
    Did whir and sparkle in the sun,
And from the first the Dodgers' woes
    Had only just begun.

"Beware the 'no windup,' my boys!
    The pitch that throws us off our pace.
Beware. The style that he employs
    Might lead us to disgrace."

Mick took his mighty glove in hand.
    Long time the long line drive he sought.
He chased it down with a backhand grab:
    Gil Hodges' smash was caught.

Frozen in time Dale Mitchell stood,
    Last hitter in the game.
Mitchell poised his stick of wood:
    The final pitch then came!

Just off the corner. Called strike three!
    And Yogi's legs went snicker-snack
Around the waist of Larsen who
    Had stilled the Bums' attack.

And hast thou slain the Bums again?
    Another Series lost, you say?
Wait till next year, Brooklyn Bums.
    O frabjous day! Callooh! Callay!

'Twas October, and Don Larsen's throws
    Did whir and sparkle in the sun,
And from the first the Dodgers' woes
    Had only just begun.

(Lewis Carroll: "Jabberwocky")

Is Our Team Winning?

"Is our team winning
   That used to dominate?
Swept four in '27,
    We did, we Yankee eight."
      Sure, we mighty Yankees
         Still seem to win somehow.
      Our Babe is big Dave Winfield;
         Dave's taller, you'll allow.
"Is shortstop handled
   Like Koenig did before?
And are there arms like Meusal's
   Around here anymore?"
      Well, we have Roy Smalley
         To go deep in the hole.
      But throwing? Steve and Jerry
         Could use a downhill roll.
"Can your first baseman
   Match what Gehrig did achieve?
Like Collins, can your catcher
   Call pitches and receive?"
      We're so stocked at catch and first
         We don't know who to keep.
      Balboni, Butch, Ken, Don, Cerone:
         Good players don't come cheap.
"At second, Lazzeri;
   At third Joe Dugan's fine —
Earle Combs to finish off the eight:
   Is your team as divine?"
      Well, at second we've got Randolph,
         And who could fill Graig's shoes?
      And big bats as DH'ers
         No way can we lose.
Mighty Yankee line-ups:
   Most powerful of men.
Who would dare to chose between
   The Yankees now and then?

(A.E. Housman: "Is My Team Ploughing?")

Note: The poem compares the 1927 Yankees to the 1982 Yankees.

Night Baseball

The bright seats in the well-filled stands;
And the yellow moon we sit below;
And the bank of lights that nightly keep
Us fans from an unwanted sleep,
As we watch our heroes hit and throw,
And we clap and shout out our commands.

Then victory nears, within our reach;
Three outs to get, and then he appears:
The ace reliever, who grabs a patch
Of glory with his game of catch,
And the stands explode with resounding cheers
Of the baseball fans' distinctive speech!

(Robert Browning: "Meeting at Night")

Artificial Grass

Watch for high bounces at Philadelphia and St. Louis,
Slap hard grounders and watch me work—
    I am artificial grass; I confound all.

And give yourself rug burns at Houston
And sore knees at Seattle and Pittsburgh.
Squeegee me off and let me work.
Two years, ten years, and fans begin to ask:
    What game is this?
    What has baseball become?

I am artificial grass.
Let me work.

(Carl Sandburg: "Grass")

Tracy Stallard

He grips the ball with shaking hands
Close to where Roger Maris stands
Bathed by the screams of hopeful fans.

Behind him are the outfield walls;
He hesitates (or is it "stalls"),
And then responds as history calls.

(Alfred Lord Tennyson: "The Eagle")

Note: According to John Blanchard, Maris was probably more nervous than Stallard; nonetheless, it was one of baseball's great moments.

Polo Hymn

In the Polo Grounds that autumn day
    The Giants' pennant flag unfurled,
Here young Bobby Thomson stood
    And hit the shot heard round the world.

The Dodgers long their lead had kept,
    The Giants had long seemed asleep.
Once thirteen back, New York had crept
    Up from that hole that seemed so deep.

From that green field, in black and white
    We share today young Thomson's leap,
Russ Hodges' shout, the fans' delight,
    Those images we'll always keep.

(Ralph Waldo Emerson: "Concord Hymn")

Bleachers

When I see Pete Rose swing both left and right
Across the years that streaked his hair with gray
I like to think some boy is still inside
And swinging with an innocence and joy
That I once felt. Surely you had those dreams
Of summer afternoons in big league parks
Swinging a bat. The tying run at first
As the pitcher winds; the ball spins and dips,
And you double home the game-winning run.
Soon the world's reality dissolves dreams,
Shattering the innocence we once knew —
Such shreds of broken dreams to sweep away
You'd think the devil must have been at work.
And then I see Rose swing both left and right
Across those years that streaked MY hair with gray.
I realize that dreams don't have to die,
That innocence and joy can still remain.
A ball park's a proper place for dreams:
I don't know where they're likely to go better.
I'd like to climb those afternoon bleachers
And eat peanuts and hot dogs and send cheers
Toward all those players who make my dreams live.
That would be good both going and coming back.
One could do worse then be a climber of bleachers.

(Robert Frost: "Birches")

Note: Written while Rose was still an active player and a symbol for the baseball dreams of millions.

Batting Against Nolan Ryan

Nolan's pitching isn't fair:
He throws a ball that isn't there.
It isn't there again today.
I wish that ball would go away.

(Hughes Means: "Antigonish")

Pete Rose Coloring His Hair

So changed! So lost! The gray withdrawn
    Which once he wore!
The sight of his gray hairs is gone
    Forevermore!

Let not black hair once short and trim
    Be gray right now.
Could Rose convey his youthful vim
    With graying brow?

Since sins have soiled glory's page,
    And honor's fled;
Keep covering that sign of age:
    A graying head.

Yes, hide your age, use rinse or dye;
    Make gray depart.
For on your head the black should lie,
    Not in your heart.

(John Greenleaf Whittier: "Ichabod")

Wrigley's Bleacher Bums

Often I think of the beautiful park
    That is seated by the lake;
Often in thoughts I do embark
To the bleachers in that treasured park
    And a joyous journey take.
        And the words the announcer shouts
        Come to my mind again:
        "They did it! Holy Cow! Cubs win!"
And thoughts of the Cubs are happy thoughts.

I can see the swing that Kingman took
    And catch, in fond recall,
The way the bleacher bums did look
On August days, our backs would cook
    Beyond the left field wall.
        And yes, those treasured shouts
        Have always made me grin:
        "They did it! Holy Cow! Cubs win!"
And thoughts of the Cubs are happy thoughts.

I remember the plays that Ernie made
    And Billy Williams' swing
(Even that ghastly Broglio trade;
And the sixty-nine late season fade);
    The wins that Sandberg helped to bring.
        Whenever spirits seem to sag
        The words come back again:
        "They did it! Holy Cow! Cubs win!"
And thoughts of the Cubs are happy thoughts.

(Henry Wadsworth Longfellow: "My Lost Youth")

Wrigley Field Neighbor

My front door lies in wait beyond
    The Wrigley's left field wall
And opens up on windy days
    To catch a long fly ball.

(Sarah N. Cleghorn: "The Golf Links")

I Never Saw the Babe

I never saw the Babe;
I never saw Ty Cobb,
Yet know I their accomplishments;
They cause my heart to throb.

I never saw a game
Played sixty years ago;
Yet in my dreams the games I see
All set my heart aglow.

(Emily Dickinson: "I Never Saw a Moor")

On First Looking at a Mantle Homer

Long had I had the pleasure to behold
The New York Yankees on the tv screen.
They played just like a powerful machine
And much good baseball drama did enfold.
Oft of Mantle's power I had been told,
But not a single home run had I seen
Which cleared the wall in Mantle's own demesne:
Death Valley, where home runs were rare as gold.
And then one day 'neath summer's sunlit skies
The Mick stepped to the plate with boyish grin
And swung; a hard line drive began to rise
Far over heads of unbelieving men,
So far that even now I realize
That I will not see Mantle's like again.

(John Keats: "On First Looking into Chapman's Homer")

The Chickenwirefence Behind My House

The chickenwirefence behind my house
is where I first
           fell in love
               with baseball
Bubblegumcards whispered stories of big leaguers
from the dry grass
A radio inside shouted through the window
                    its Sunday baseball
           and base hits
        and Oh boy Homers

Outside I stood beyond the fence and pitched

My pitches had minds of their own

A target too small
For the wild throws
Of an eight year old trying to be Feller

Yet the bubblegum cards nearby
               urged me on
                   Someday! Someday!

(Lawrence Ferlinghetti: "The Pennycandystore Beyond the El")

Note: Cleveland's ace, Bob Feller.

To Dale Murphy

Murphy, thy image is to me
  Like Aaron's in the days of yore,
An absolute consistency,
   A classic swing the fans adore,
   And home runs by the score.

On outside fields or in the dome,
   You play the game with strength and grace:
On outfield grasses where you roam
   Diving catches do not cease
Nor do perfect strikes to home.

Oh! when the hurler starts to pitch
   My heart beats wildly as you stand
   With magic bat within thy hand!
I follow you and find my niche—
   In wonderland!

(Edgar Allan Poe: "To Helen")

Waiting Out a Player Strike

To him who in the love of baseball holds
Communion with her visible forms, she speaks
A various language; for his gayer hours
She has a voice of gladness as the crowd
At Wrigley takes its seventh inning stretch:
And as she glides into his darker musings
Sees the sorrow of all those players
To whom the fates were less than kind.

When thoughts of baseball strikes come like a blight
Over thy spirit, and sad thoughts of long
Summer days with empty big league ballparks
Fill you with dismay, think of all the feats
Of yesterday that still will bring you joy.

Our thoughts go down the path to walk with all
The patriarchs of a previous time—
With bowlegged Honus riding herd at short,
With despised Ty, spikes scissoring the air,
With Big Train pouring fastballs, with Sam Rice
Leaping into outfield seats to save
A World Series game—walking with thousands
Past the players who now sit in strike-caused
Loneliness while we dream of what has been.

Let us go, soothed by unfaltering trust,
Into summer, and let today's stars play,
So that the innumerable caravan
Of baseball stars walks down paths of glory
Somewhere in the future, and names will be
Those who would be playing now, and those who
Will play tomorrow, and bring pleasant dreams.

(William Cullen Bryant: "Thanatopsis")

The Lead Rises, the League Falls

The lead rises, the league falls,
As White Sox hitters start blasting balls
And shutting opposition down
In each A.L. contending town,
    And the lead rises, the league falls.

Long balls land on the roofs and walls,
And when LaRussa to the bullpen calls,
A reliever comes and understands
The dreams he holds within his hands.
    And the lead rises, the league falls.

The crowd demands some encore calls
For batters hitting home run balls;
The season ends, but not before
The fans share in a victory roar
    As the lead rises, the league falls.

(Henry Wadsworth Longfellow: "The Tide Rises, the Tide Falls")

Note: Written in 1983, when the Tony LaRussa–led White Sox blew away the rest of the league, beating the second place Royals by 20 games.

The Curve Ball

Break, break, break,
    On the black of home plate, O Curve!
And the ump will perchance call "Strike!"
    If only he has the nerve.

O well for the rifle-armed ace,
    Who brings home a superstar's pay!
O well for the wild-high fastballer,
    Who keeps all the hitters at bay!

And hitters swing as in darkness
    When the flamethrower's on the hill,
But when junk pitchers don't get the corners,
    The hitters dig in for the kill.

Break, break, break,
    Oh my heart when the ump shouts, "Ball!"
For the glory I dreamed of will soon be dead
    When my curve ball won't get the ump's call.

(Alfred Lord Tennyson: "Break, Break, Break")

Ricky Henderson

Ricky stole a base today,
Broke Cobb's mark along the way.
No longer is Ricky the pursuer,
And that's one record chase the fewer.

(Henry Graham: "Grandpapa")

When I Saw the Learn'd Computer

When I saw the learn'd computer,
When its printout, its decision, was spread out before me,
When I was shown who hits what pitcher, what buttons to
    push to win games,
When I saw the computer make all my decisions for me with
    its irrefutable logic,
How tired I became and fell into sleep,
Till dreams came of the computer telling Miller Huggins
Not to play Babe Ruth against certain left-handers,
And I thought of how the computer could have silenced the stars.

(Walt Whitman: "When I Heard the Learn'd Astronomer")

Those Bases on Balls

Something there is that doesn't love a ball,
That makes has-beens of would-be pitching stars
And finds me in the dugout pulling hair
And phoning to the bullpen for relief.
The work of hitters is another thing:
I've watched them — artists with a stick of wood
As they knocked home runners from every base
Against a seasoned veteran's strongest pitch —
A slider, down and in. The walks I mean,
No manager can bear to see them made,
But almost every game I see them there.
I meet my pitcher out upon the hill
When all the bases have been filled by walks
And start to send him to the showers once again.
He keeps the ball and will not let it go.
To each the burden that has fallen to each.
My pitcher has thrown so many walks
That the game is now in the balance:
"You're coming out; you cannot find the plate."
I wear my psyche rough with handling him.
Oh, managing is just a game of wits,
One on a side, it comes to little more:
Some pitching mound psychology:
He is too sensitive; I am too harsh.
If I could keep from yelling quite so much
His control would be okay, he tells me.
He only says, "Good managers are more patient."
There is no mischief in me, but I wonder
If I could put a notion in his head:
"If I were not so patient you would be
Back picking apples on a Vermont farm.
Before I'd go and walk another man
I'd think about the consequence and know
To whom I might be like to give offense.
Something there is that doesn't love a ball,
That wants a strike." I could say more to him,
But what could I say that has not been said,
That he couldn't say himself? I see him there,
Grasping the ball firmly across the seams
In his left hand, like Koufax in his prime.
His hand begins to sweat, it seems to me,
And memories of Koufax disappear.
He will not go beyond his foolish saying,
And he likes having thought of it so well
He says again, "Good managers are more patient."

(Robert Frost: "Mending Wall")

Timeclock

To what purpose, April, do you return again?
Football is not enough.
It can no longer excite me with the crashing
Of shoulder pads and cracking of helmets.
I know what I love —
The pastoral splendor of baseball, where time
Stretches to fit the game.
The lack of a clock is good.
It is apparent that there is no rush.
What does football's clock signify?
A frenzied mass of confusion, or worse yet
Hopeless last minutes.
Spring by itself
Is nothing,
It needs baseball, with its flight of timeless fancy.
It is not enough that yearly, with new leagues,
Football
Comes like an idiot, ticking toward its destruction.

(Edna St. Vincent Millay: "Spring")

Free Agent

From the voice of his agent came the plea,
And the player could not help but hark to him:
And bank accounts soon filled to the brim,
And the fans all sighed for what used to be.

(Robert Browning: "Parting at Morning")

Casey and the Agent

Bad King Kong Carl Casey got his nickname one spring day
When he drilled three balls (like Kingman did one afternoon at Shea)
Which might have gone in orbit far above the modern park
Had not the domed roof stopped each drive before it reached its arc.

Some baseball fans thought he was greater than the Babe or Cobb,
But Casey knew no history; baseball was just a job.
When legendary names were whispered, and their merits weighed,
Bad Casey's only question was, "How much did they get paid?"

He wouldn't talk to teammates, would ignore a coach's sign,
And then, when questioned by the press would never once decline
To rant and rave about some bonehead play a teammate made,
And moan and mutter oaths about how he was underpaid.

He hit .420 his third year and won the home run crown.
In the voting for the MVP, Bad Casey won hands down.
His agent then approached him with some fatherly advice:
"The owner's pie is huge," he said. "Go for a bigger slice.

"Hold out for more," the agent said. "Let's make them guarantee
Three million bucks a year for life, and if they won't agree
Then go on strike until the owners recognize the worth
Of King Kong Carl Casey, the best ball player on earth."

And King Kong Carl Casey dreamed of all that he could buy
With the large and juicy hunk of his wealthy owner's pie.
He stayed at home to check his mail when teammates headed South.
The only exercise he got was shooting off his mouth.

Days turned to weeks and still he waited, growing mad and fat;
And yet until they paid him, he refused to swing a bat.
No check arrived; no teammates called to beg Bad Casey back.
"Their loss," Bad Casey muttered, "for I'm their whole attack."

"They've got no other hitters, and their runners all are slow."
The season started; his old team won twelve games in a row.
A light began to flicker in his mind, and slowly spread,
So Casey phoned his agent, and in desperation said:

"I've listened long enough, old buddy, to the likes of you;
I think it's time we compromised; two million bucks will do.
Call the owner; make your pitch. I think it's pretty plain
That all of baseball will be thrilled to see me once again."

Oh, somewhere in this favored land, glad Little Leaguers play
A game for fun which Major Leaguers grumble at for pay.
That baseball will survive Bad Casey, there seems little doubt,
For King Kong Carl Casey's greedy agent has struck out.

(Ernest Thayer: "Casey at the Bat")

Note: This was written before the advent of million dollar a year contracts (and before the spiraling effects of the collusion rulings).

Part Three:
The Players

Henry Aaron

Some hated him
merely because
he did not, like Clemente,
have the good grace to die
before the hallowed marks
were broken.
Instead,
in that historic carnival
where Kuhn, Downing, House
shared brief moments of
(in) fame (y),
he stilled the whispered threats
of
death.

Harry Agganis

Disease
must love first basemen,

but this one had no
        special "day"
no
        "luckiest man" speech
no
        biographies
no
        movies or tv plays
                        to sing
his praise,

no "Iron Horse" this,
just a "Golden Greek"
who died
            into
            oblivion.

Dick Allen

They threw garbage in his yard,
called him a troublemaker,
sent him from

      city
        to
      city

The media   s   h
                      t   i
                      r   m
                      i
                      p   d
                      p   o
                      e   w
                      d   n

looked for horns or hooves,
knocked him for not playing
on a brok-en/leg.

He seemed to want only
to take his quarter million
a year and

          like Gulliver

be left alone
with his horses.

Jesus Alou

that crick in his
neck

never seemed to

go away it

didn't run in the

family

tho maybe

he got too

closetoclemente and he

caught it all

I know is that it made me

nervous just

looking at him

Ernie Banks

Quick wrists and "It's a great day to play two!"
and baseball became a game again.
He flowed at shortstop until legs failed,
but the wrists stayed strong
through more than five hundred homers.
Twice MVP, he stayed eternally optimistic
through a career on a team with eleven
straight second division finishes.
Universally loved,
baseball's ambassador,
he always made us smile.
Selfishly, we were glad no one
made him a manager:
symbols are in greater demand.

Yogi Berra

"You don't hit a baseball
with your face," he said
when accused of not being pretty.
He could hit good and bad
pitches hard enough
that looks didn't matter.
He'd as likely hit a home run
as strike out; "the best clutch
hitter in the game," many said.
It's never been over for Yogi,
not on The Hill, not with the Yankees,
not with the Mets or the Astros.
Some men retire, some die;
memory fades with passing years.
With Yogi, it'll never be over.

Ewell Blackwell

Almost matching Vandermeer's
feat, his pitches

— — —whippedin— — —

from the general direction

***of**
* third*
**base*

making right handers

d
i
v
e   for cover

from strikes

or at least make them wish
that their dads, like Mickey's,
had forced them to switchhit.

Steve Blass

His hold on fame
was as tight as a child's grip
on a soap bubble blown
in spring's nippy breezes.
When the plate started moving
itwaslikepitchingonthedeadrun
or from an escalator going down,
down from World Series hero
to minor league has-been.
Too fast, that escalator
that held the man we knew as Blass,
the best we knew of class.

Ken Boyer

consistency was his trademark. day in-
day out, year after year, his statist-
ics never varied enough to notice. few
played a better third base (maybe his
brother, over in the other league, and
brooks, at baltimore). spectacular
enough to be the league's mvp once, he
was great all the time, an all-star.
consistency was his trademark. day in-
day out, year after year, his statist-

Lew Burdette

He perfected the


```
        u
    e  o s   mannerisms
  n rv
```

long before Gaylord.
He distracted the Yankees enough
in the '57 Series to almost match
Mathewson's '05 feat. Threw a
wonderful alleged   spi
                        tt
                           er.

For us Yankee fans it was easy
to see how he succeeded.

To hold a Yankee team of Berra
and Howard and Mantle and Bauer
scoreless for 24 straight innings,

to win 163 games in a 10-year stretch
is easy: anyone can do it with the


```
                u
  right      e  o s      mannerisms.
           n rv
```

Jim Brosnan

A good enough reliever to write a book,
he wrote one good enough to sell another,
funny enough to make Solly Hemus miserable.
He showed fans
(long before Marvin Miller and Jim Bouton)
that players are not gods
and that some are as literate
as human beings are.

Dean Chance

Some said Bo held him back,
even though he got Cy Young once,
won twenty twice.
Amateur psychologists
wanted to tell him
who his friends should be.
No one seemed to worry about Belinsky
squandering his OWN talent,
sensing the irrefutable truth
that some southpaws are too far gone
for help.
When Dean retired into ranching
for awhile, no one was surprised
when Bo didn't come along
as hired hand.

Roger Clemens

High Heat.
Other than Ryan,
who heats it up
as well?

High Heat
brings the numbers:
11 k's, 3 hits,
a shutout.

High Heat
up around the eyes;
no way can they
stop their swings

High Heat
gets there so quick.
Sure, there are curves,
too, but it was

High Heat
that once struck out
20 in a game,
and it is

High Heat
that stopped a Bosox
losing streak 36 times
in 42 tries.

High Heat
saved the Sox
in their late collapse
in '90.

High Heat
almost always keeps
the Bosox from going
cold.

Rocky Colavito

hisboomingbatlikea

= = = = = = = = = = = = = = c

howitzeraimedatthe

P
i
t
c
h
e
r

was powerful enough to

" " " " " "
"   "
"   "
"   B L A S T   "
"   "
"   "
" " " " " "

FOUR home runs a game

once

at Baltimore
of all places

Gavvy Cravath

Someday, a long time from now,
when time has lifted all the sluggers
into their eternal rest to meet
for a heavenly round of Home Run Derby
with Mark Scott, the pairings will be set:

Hank Aaron	vs.	Mickey Mantle
Frank Robinson	vs.	Mike Schmidt
Willie Mays	vs.	Reggie Jackson
Gavvy Cravath	vs.	Harmon Killebrew

Go ahead, choose Aaron with his 755.
Or Mantle with his mammoth blows from both sides,
a man strong enough to come within inches
of hitting a fair ball out of Yankee Stadium.
Take Mays, he's no slouch with 660,
one of only four men to top 50 more than once.
You might think the 500-plus of Jackson or Schmidt
or Robinson or Killebrew will win for you.
Go ahead. It's fine with me.

I'll take the Phillies' outfielder,
the man whose batted ball hit a seagull
and a Spanish-speaking spectator screamed,
"Gaviota! Gaviota!" Seagull. Seagull.
I'll take my chances with the only man
in this group of sluggers to lead his league
in home runs six times in seven years.
Go ahead. Take your Aaron or Mantle or Mays.
Settle for the runners-up: Killebrew
or Robinson or Jackson or Schmidt.
I'll beat you with Gavvy.

Rob Deer

On the occasion of a miraculous
Brewers win

Classic baseball.
the kind dreams are made of.
Or fiction.
But sometimes the fiction
is real
and the dreams come true
for some
and turn into nightmares
for others.

Reardon, ahead 4–3,
last of the ninth,
one on, two out.
Deer has fanned three times
already.
He fouls off
four pitches
until he gets one
he can handle.

We scoff at a script so trite,
so manipulated.

We thrill at the unbelievability
of reality.

Joe DiMaggio

You transformed   a baseball field
   into   a work of art.

You played with the   form
   and   grace
     and   strength
       and   intensity

of   Ravel
   or   Hemingway
     or   Arthur Miller
       or   George Bellows

your glory is our glory
your sorrow is our sorrow
your humanness is our humanness

Our hearts fill with pity
       for those millions
           who know you
     only
as a hustler
   of coffee

Ryne Duren

He rifled the ball high
against the backstop,
his glasses flying off
into
the
dust.
Crawling on hands and knees,
searching for the thick lenses,
blind and hungover,
he frightened the hitter
into a cold sweat.
Unknowing fans thought him a hero;
knowing fans know him a hero
who stopped crawling in the dust.
They watched him stand taller than fame.

Nellie Fox

Long before cancer
we feared that he would swallow
that huge chaw and hurt himself.
He could spit about as far
as he hit the ball,
but he always hit it somewhere.
He struck out as often
as Billy Pierce won a game,
about three times a month
(one reason WHY Billy won
his three a month).
With one out and a man on third,
he was your man:
we knew it,
Pierce knew it,
Paul Richards and Marty Marion
and Al Lopez surely knew it.
We knew we could count on Nellie.

Joe Garagiola

He could catch (sometimes)
and could tell stories (always),
a more fortunate circumstance
than merely being able
to catch, throw, hit,
run, or hit with power.

We should all be so bad,
to hit .316 in a World Series
at the age of 20, his rookie year,
back in '46, the same year he
virtually matched the stats
of teammate Harry "The Hat" Walker.
(Nobody ever said Walker couldn't hit.)

But it's easier to joke
about incompetence than skill,
so, to hear Joe tell it, it's good
he played for Pittsburgh when he did,
when a successful road trip
was
ten days
of rain.

Bruce Gardner Returns to the Mound

College pitcher of the year in 1960,
an arm injury cut short a promising pro career

All alone, gun
in hand,
I stalk
the mound—
the sacred ground
where once
I pitched
and won.

But future glory
never came.
The game I lived for
passed me by.
I return here—
the only place
I truly loved—
to die.

Paul Giel

The wrong Giants signed him
after those glory years
on the Minnesota gridiron.
When the hitters started hanging
onto his pitches as easily
as his receivers had done,
he did the only sensible thing.
The Golden Gophers seemed glad
to see him again,
the conquered hero
come home.

The Emergence of Kelly Gruber, Spring, 1989

He was good coming in.
The top ten in hitting:
some key RBI.
But who would have expected
this kind of day:
six ribbies,
the first Blue Jay in history
to hit for the cycle
("The last hit was the toughest,"
he said. "If it looks like extra bases,
do I go for two or stop at first
and look silly?"),
instrumental in fighting back
from an 8–1 disadvantage.

Say "Blue Jay" yesterday,
the echo bounces back:
Steib, Bell, McGriff.

Say "Blue Jay" tomorrow
and the world thunders:
"Gruber."

Frank Howard

```
                 vv      dd
The ground    qq ii  ee  ee        when he ran.
              uu      rr
```

On the college basketball court,
no one thought him a   GG
                         II
                         AA
                         NN
                         TT
                         TT
                         TT

On a baseball field, he seemed

                              out of place,
the bat like a   t
                    o
                    o
                    t
                    h
                    p
                    i
                    c
                    k

in his hands.
No miracle man, he gave the best he had.
The baseball world was glad
he decided to hit home runs
instead of load boxes in Green Bay.

Harvey Haddix

No one ever pitched a better game
and lost.
His only consolation
was that his team's incompetence
with the bats
gave him a chance
to pitch three more innings
than Larsen, Catfish,
and the rest.
Compared to a meow, his was a purr,
but his feat gave him
the next best thing to nine lives:
immortality.

Ken Hubbs

Like Clemente,
he died in a plane crash,
but Roberto had already earned
a Hall of Fame berth,
while he only had potential.
His fielding record for second basemen
made Cub fans forget Baker,
before he too was forgotten
after being waived
out of the league
by that frozen Utah lake.

Catfish Hunter

*Obtained by the Yankees in 1975
as the first and most expensive
of the free agents of his era*

$$$$ Not many $$$$ pitchers were $$$$
better over $$$$ a period $$$$ of time
$$$$ that brought $$$$ three straight $$$$
World Championships, $$$$ a perfect $$$$ game,
twenty $$$$ wins five $$$$ years in $$$$ a row,
$$$$ the Hall $$$$ of Fame. $$$$ Even a $$$$
broken finger $$$$ from that $$$$ All-Star
game $$$$ couldn't stop $$$$ him. $$$$ Charley
couldn't $$$$ stop him $$$$ and diabetes $$$$
couldn't stop $$$$ him and $$$$ since all $$$$
the Yankees' $$$$ didn't stop $$$$ him it
$$$$ turned out $$$$ that only $$$$ time could
stop. $$$$
him

Bo Jackson

On opening day, 1989

He did everything but win.
Led a seventh inning rally, then,
last of the ninth —
Kansas City down 4–3 —
Bo delivers, a hard ground ball
to center, splitting the distance
between the bag and second baseman.

Routine.

Except: the centerfielder comes over and in,
makes a clean play, a quick play,
fires to second.
AND BO IS THERE ALREADY! sliding
before the sweep of tag.

An out later, with Bo on third,
almost anything (fly ball, error, wild pitch)
will tie the game.
That White strikes out, the Royals lose,
seems anticlimatic.

For Bo serves notice
that Bo will be noticed:
    a streak.
    a blur.
    a human missile
    exploding
    across our incredulous
    sight.

Jackie Jensen

An rbi leader with
speed,
power,
the Splendid Splinter
batting ahead of him,
all he needed
for the Hall of Fame
was to rid himself
of his fear of flying.
Long before Erica Jong,
we speculated that he retired early
because his wife
in a bathing suit
looked better than the Splendid Splinter
in full uniform
any day.

Al Kaline

That great nickname
"Salty"
never caught on.

Not colorful enough for nicknames,
he played without one,
without fanfare.

Stepping into the big leagues
without pro experience,
he won a batting title

younger than anyone else,
established himself as a star
with glove, arm, bat.

Until only the bat remained,
swinging methodically
past the 3,000 hit mark.

So smooth.
So quiet.
So good.

Paul Kilgus

Under Wrigley Field lights
in early April

Kilgus didn't seem to mind the cold,
taking a shutout into the ninth,
until Burnanski's homer.
So, all in all, I guess
getting lights paid off.

Now the school kids have somewhere to go
on freezing April nights
with the wind chill six degrees off the lake.
Bundled under blankets, smothered
by winter coats,
Wrigley Field patrons are a throwback
to the old days:
Ice Age Baseball.

We expected night games in July, August,
to keep players fresh for a pennant drive.

We were foolish.
We forgot about the bottom line,
which means fans in the stands —
now.
School kids, freezing under blankets
in the chill
of a leftover
winter
wind.

Ted Kluszewski

His arms were tree trunks with hair.
With his sleeveless shirt
he looked like a misplaced blacksmith.
Dizzy Dean told us that sawdust
dripped from the bat when Klu squeezed it.
We, the fans, laughed, but not
the opposing outfielders,
amateur mountain climbers
on that old Crosly Field terrace.

Duel with Gary Kolb

No household name, yours,
even though you chalked up
seven-plus big league seasons.
I wish you'd been a superstar,
so I could brag about
that pre–big league game in 1958
when we played opposing center fields,
my only game ever against
a present, past, or future big leaguer.
I outhit you 2 to 1,
and I won the game 1 to 0
when I challenged your rifle arm,
trucking from second on a single to center,
sliding headfirst into home,
better than Pete Rose long before
Pete made the world bow.
Your lack of stardom cost me
reflected glory, Gary Kolb.
Nobody cares now about my 1958
successful dash from second to home.
No one but me.

Sandy Koufax

Nothing anyone could write
    Could fully recreate the sight
Of Sandy Koufax in his prime.

Nothing anyone could say
    Could make us see the magic way
His pitches came, time after time

To make the hitters swing through air.
    Our picture of what happened there
Would be a lame facsimile.

The pitcher's mound was Sandy's book
    And every sweep his left arm took
Composed a line of poetry.

It's Sandy's poems that make us thrill,
    The ones he wrote with unmatched skill
Those last six years of his career.

He read to us from every page
    While on the baseball field, his stage.
We hear him yet, and rise, and cheer.

Tony Kubek

He went down like he'd been shot.
Maz can thank that bad hop
for eternal fame,
for that storybook ending
he wrote back in '60
that went over the head of Yogi Berra.

The back hurt more than
the Adam's apple did,
so Tony became a graduate of YIBS
(Yankee
Infielders'
Broadcasting
School),
surprising us all in '67 by converting
a hopeless World Series tv assignment
into personal triumph.

Second fiddle?
Maybe.
But I never tired of the melody.

Frank Lary

If only all teams
had been as mighty as the Yankees,
as easy to beat, he might have been
the greatest pitcher in Tiger history.
Safe in his reputation as Yankee killer,
he merely tossed his glove on the mound,
listened gleefully to the Yankees' #$&%*%!
and told Charlie "Paw Paw" Maxwell
to hit a game-winning home run.

Vance Law

Life's embarrassing moments.
Even the best have them.
A chance to beat the Doc,
15-3 against the Cubs lifetime
going in.
The Cubs score early,
lead 3-0 in the fifth.

Then it happens . . .
the object lesson for parents
and Little League coaches
all over the country:
a pop-up to Law at third
with two outs —
the inning will be over —
he stands, waits,
waits,
sticks up his glove;
the ball hits it,
pops out

POPS OUT!

His right hand is off somewhere
daydreaming
while the ball

POPS OUT OF HIS GLOVE!

The Mets score.
And all over the country
parents yell at their children:
"Two hands! See what happens
when you don't use two hands!"

But no one listens nowadays.
The Doc is 16-3 against the Cubs.
And at least part of the reason
is a pop-up to third
and a daydreaming
right hand.

Phil Linz

His glove had glue
but he might as well have hit with a
(the only player to help
win a pennant with a)
harmonica.
He might have starred
with someone (anyone) else
but preferred ("play me or pay me")
to stay.
When the checks stopped,
he did
too

I, McCovey

After the 1962 World Series

The sinking sun throws dusky, silent shadows
across the empty field,
across empty stands where once thousands cheered
and thousands cried,
witnesses to my final drive of futility.

I stand alone thinking how close I came to making
Terry the new Branca, to having
my name immortalized; like Thomson I would become
a legend in my own prime.
Just empty dreams, shattered now.

Denny McLain

A modern Tantalus.
His Hall of Fame plaque
within his grasp.

We all looked for excuses;
when wins declined,
we studied him off the field:
his passion for Pepsi,
his supposed talent at the organ,
his avocation as a pilot,
gamblers,
bankruptcy,
juvenile pranks.

A hard man to believe,
his explanation seemed too simple,
a rejection of Aristotle
and hubris and the tragic flaw
when he said: "My arm went dead."

Sal Maglie

Jack the Ripper seemed safer
than Bozo the Clown
next to unshaven Sal.
Batters shivered,
knowing that he preferred
shaving others closer than himself.
He would snarl
whenever that pitcher's rubber
touched his foot.

Mickey Mantle

A mummy in pinstripes.
Power dripped from taped muscles.
Tapes measured massive drives
that hung in the air longer
than the interviews he hated to give.
Pain chased him forever
faster than his dash to first
on left-handed drag bunts,
clouded his boyish country grin,
forced him to face himself
in a future as spectator.
Years after retirement,
he said he still dreams of playing,
of his getting the big hit.
So do we, Mickey. So do we.

Juan Marichal

the leg high above the head
like a child starting to fall backward
from a picnic table,
but always in control
except once at bat (embarrassing)

he finished his career
with no worse than the fifth best
winning percentage in history,
and he never once
fell off the table

138

Billy Martin

We've heard your life summed up,
even trivialized with a scattering
of names, words, phrases:

marshmallows, martinis,
Mantle and Reedy,
Reggie and George.

Oakland and Billyball.
Jim Brewer and Dave Boswell.
Art Fowler and George Weiss.

Casey Stengel.
Throwing dirt.
Number 1.

Yet there's one phrase that speaks
louder than all the rest:
"Jackie Robinson's pop-up,"

A moment in time that speaks
the word that describes you best:
"Winner."

Willie Mays

Leo's boy.
Fans loved him
not only for his super skill
but for youthful exuberance.
His head couldn't hold a cap,
couldn't keep his voice from squeaking,
but it could think like a computer
in center field
and on the bases.
Leo made him quit stickball
in his prime.
We felt saddened
in his last year when he dropped
a fly ball. God
isn't supposed to slow down.

Willy Miranda

two throws in spring training
and the arm was loose,

the bat never did unwind,
stayed tight
his whole career

so that when
we checked averages   but not far
in Sunday's paper   reading upward,
we just started . . . . at the bottom,

Don Mossi — Ray Narleski

left   and   right
they made relief pitching
respectable

"the gold dust twins"

before people had any inkling
that relief pitchers
were not just
                    h

                    a

                    n

              ger's-o

                        n

or second-raters

not good enough to start
just bad enough to throw
to
the
wolves

The Death of Thurman Munson

1976 World Series,
Bench and Sparky on mound:
"He can flat-out hit!"
followed by line single to right

my mind still sees his quick release,
almost sidearmed to second, slicing
throws like shanked three-irons of duffers,
yet killing rallies as if by power of will

pseudo-surly, the new "scrap-iron,"
playing hurt like Fisk, Bench,
fellow winners whose value is measured
by more than their all-impressive numbers

my sons met me at airport, holding
evening paper with headlines: "Munson Dead";
baseball died a little that day,
but then, as always, was reborn,

even magnified in heard voices
on old World Series films —
respectful, almost awed voices:
"He can flat-out hit!"

Dale Murphy

Off to a slow start in the 1989 season

Twenty at-bats, no ribbies.
a chance for redemption:
two down in the twelfth, two on, two out—
a homer wins it.
Except for the extra innings,
just like Casey 100 years ago,
Mudville's savior.

Our hearts harden at the sight
of a futile swing at a curve
low and away,
a rookie-type swing,
unworthy of a former MVP.

Our hearts see what the eyes will not,
the Murphy of old,
the long drive out of the park.
He takes a fast ball
on the outside corner.

It ends not with a bang,
not even with a whimper.
Simply
silence.

Stan Musial

No
one
copied
his
little

      i   e
  w   g   l
       g

nor found the way to
copy
his

  for
       + for = HITTING
  mula

If the legs
had cooperated,
he
could
have
hit

  F   O   R   E   V   E   R

Ron Northey

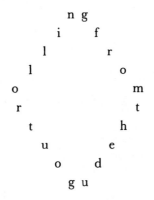

```
        n g
    i       f
  l           r
  l             o
o                 m
  r               t
    t           h
      u       e
        o   d
        g u
```

he grabbed a bat.
The rules were   OGRWN
for him.

   With
designated   runners
designated   fielders,
his bat might have carried him
to the Hall of Fame
.   (or All-Star Game, at least)

Since pitchers would rather win
2–1 than lose
5–4, he rode the bench.
He borrowed a glove
to play right field once,
and he almost got

                          lost.

Satchel Paige

He might have pitched

forever

if Boston hadn't   bunted.
Brought to Cleveland to get
          his pension,
he surprised skeptics who
didn't believe   in

```
           *
     a  *  i
     t  *  n
     n  *  o
     u  *  f
     o  *  y
     f  *  o
     the uth
```

When we wanted to think of
          "what might of been"
he called out from his

          rockingchair

and told us

          not to.

Camilo Pascual

The

B I G G E S T

      C
   U
R   in baseball
   V
     E

b
  e
  n
t   .

      a
   d   r
    Griffith
    Stadium.
   n   o
     u

The Philadelphia Three, Plus One

For Judy Palladinetti

Their autographed picture arrived this morning,
the four of them before their golf match:
Bobby Shantz, Curt Simmons, Robin Roberts, Jack Brown,
reviving memories of the 1950's
when I dreamed my way through diagramming sentences,
through elementary algebraic equations,
waiting for THE SPORTING NEWS, for Saturday's
Game of the Week, Sunday's radio baseball,
for All-Star games and the World Series,
heroes showing me what I myself might someday do.
    The uniforms in today's picture are knit shirts
    and shorts or slacks of middle-aged golfers
    to whom the tiny, flagged hole cut from the curved green
    beyond the fairway bunkers, water, and tree-lined rough
    must seem as menacing as Mantle or Williams
    or the Duke or Stan the Man
    or Willie waving lumber sixty feet away.
How can they remember as clearly as I
those days so quickly gone:
the way Bobby sprang from the mound on bunts,
his three straight strikeouts in the '52 All-Star Game
before rain washed away his chance to match Hubbell's feat,
that 1960 bad hop off Kubek's throat behind him;
Curt's 18 clutch wins in '64, his World Series
duel against Bouton, his league leading
six shutouts when he was only 23;
Robin's 1950 pennant-clinching game against the Dodgers,
his 28–7 record for an otherwise five hundred team,
his courageous finesse pitching with the Cubs,
battling to reach that unreachable 300th win —
too many memories to name, some painful, some Godlike feats
that cannot be reduced to words invented by mortals.
    They tossed 96 shutouts, won 598 big league games,
    but Jack Brown is my current hero:
    it is because of him and through his daughter Judy
    that the autographed picture came today,
    a photo to renew memories of long-ago years
    spent dreaming my way through school
    where chalk clicked on chalkboards
    like catcher's mitts cracking
    from the powerful pitches of the Philadelphia Three.

Jimmy Piersall

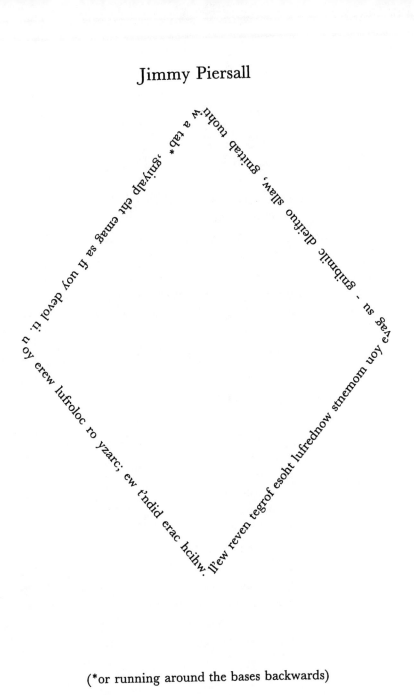

(*or running around the bases backwards)

Reese and Rizzuto

Marbles make me think of spring,
scooters — summer, somehow, kids free from school
and speeding along quiet sidewalks,
swerving to miss housewives with grocery bags.

The two together make me think of October,
of shortstops dueling in Ebbets Field,
in the late afternoon shadows of Yankee Stadium,
while we argued who was better, Reese or Rizzuto.

Only fans of the Dodgers and Yankees knew. For the
rest of us it was a coin flip, like choosing between
two words with almost the same meaning. Astounding or
Amazing. Incandescent or Luminous. Rizzuto or Reese.

Jim Rivera

His headfirst slides
electrified fans
long before Pete Rose
made the bigs.
With Minoso,
a fearsome twosome.
Stolen bases are more exciting
than home runs,
but he could get both.
He lived in a dirty uniform,
and his earlier trouble
with the law was forgotten
when the Windy City dust
started to fly.

Phil Rizzuto

He could squeeze them home
by bunting the ball off his ear.
Mistaken for a batboy,

    he
    was
    a
    giant
    in
    pin-
    stripes,
    pro-
    viding
    eter-   short
    nal   kid
    hope   on
    for   the
    the   block.

Robin Roberts

Noted for gopher balls,
     pinpoint   (50)   control,
and   (100)   wins,

we all thought it a   (125)
    shame he toiled for
the   (150)   Phillies

when we all knew the Yankees
    would   (175)   give him
thirty wins every year.

He never   (200)   complained,
    at least not so we could tell,
even   (225)   went back

to the minors,   (250)   hoping
    to get back for that three hundredth
win. Writers who kept him waiting

for five   (275)   years for the Hall
    forgot that for a long time
no one was   (286)   better.

Brooks Robinson

The human vacuum cleaner
ran slow, moved quick!
No Hall of Famer ever
could charge a bunt
so suddenly still
on the long green grass
halfway to third
and throw with his fist
almost touching the ground,
then slouch toward roars of fans
still thrilled by miracles.

Pete Rose

"What's in a name? A Rose by
any other name would hit .300"

Shakespeare's lines still ring true
today (what they call your "universality")

though Willy wasn't a baseball fan
didn't know the difference

between second base and left field,
between third base and first base

or between a low-priced singles hitter
and a million dollar home run slugger

still, when he wrote his
"a rose by any other name"

he knew what he was talking
about, all right

Pete Rose

*Further reports emerge
that he has bet on his own team*

Character.
All over the sports pages.
In headlines.
Hidden in interviews:
"We're going to ride Abbott hard,
mock his deformity, see if he can handle it."
Drugs.
Alcohol.
Adultery.
Greed.

Gambling.

On baseball?
On his own team?

We remember most the intensity —
that sprint to first after a base on balls,
the headfirst slide ("you can see the ball better
and get your picture in the papers more"),
the near fight after striking out on a
Phil Regan alleged spitter,
the scrap with Bud Harrelson,
the 44-game hitting streak.

Intensity.
Charles Hustle.
Always the intensity.
Few have given so much to baseball.
If rumors prove true,
few will have taken so much away.

Nolan Ryan

On the occasion of a near no-hitter, April 12, 1989

When will it end,
that fast ball mowing down hitters
in the cradle when he started
with the Mets.
A perfect game into the seventh,
no-hitter in the eighth,
15 K's.

I thought he might get it,
(even without the curve),
this chilly Wisconsin night.
For the change was working for him,
and against the blinding heat
from his 42-year-old arm,
who could hit him?
Francona is all;
at least the hit was a solid one,
a liner over third,
no fluke to rob him of his sixth gem.
He left after eight innings,
134 pitches, most of them strikes.
Sure, relief help would have been nice —
a third combined one-hitter
to add to his nine solo ones —
but it wasn't to be.
No matter.
He's still here, thrilling us,
shooting for no-hitters.
And it wouldn't surprise me
to see him,
even now,
get another one.

Nolan Ryan

He threw a white pea
fast faster faster fastest
of them all,
Try hitting a pea
with a toothpick
and you'll see what it's like
to bat against the
fast faster faster fastest
of them all.

Nolan Ryan

Another near no-hitter, April 23, 1989

Every time out
there's a chance
for another one.
Every few minutes, the update:
"A no-hitter after five...
no hits into the seventh...
the eighth..."

Then: "Liriano tripled
with one out
in the ninth."

42-years-old.
And getting better.

How do we measure
the greatest of them all?
30, 40 years from now
our grandchildren, great-grandchildren
will come to us,
a hint of awe in their voices,
their eyes wide:
"Did you really see Ryan pitch?
Did you, Gramps?"

Hank Sauer

With Kiner, he provided power
but made Baumholtz work.
If he wasn't bad defensively,
sports writers have been fibbing
about him all these years.
Cub fans remember fondly
those years of futility
when occasionally he not only
brightened their day
with a long home run, but
also gave them a few lau(ha)ghs.

Herb Score

Until his comet lit Cleveland's skies,
no one ever struck out so many so soon.
His speed and control
let us know that he would be
one of the greats.

We can still see Rocky
putting his glove
under
his
head

as the bloody face
      lay   swelling
on the dust of the mound.
(If it's any consolation,
Gil was thrown out.)

Bobby Shantz

Too small to be a great pitcher,
he became outstanding.
He helped Philadelphia
live down W. C. Fields'
disparaging line,
pounced on bunts
better than a cat could,
came within a rainout
of Hubbell's All-Star Game
feat, showed us that an arm
doesn't have to be long to be good.

Enos Slaughter

St. Louis—
the cap
lasting longer than hair
pushes summers across
his forehead,
hot summers of hitting,
of defense,
of hustle
toward that call:
HALL OF FAME
HAll of FAme,
Hall of Fame,
hall of fame,
hall of,
hall,
ha... ha... ha...

Note: After years of disappointment, Enos Slaughter was belatedly named to the Hall of Fame in 1985, 26 years after his retirement from baseball.

Roy Smalley

Being in the wrong city
at the wrong time
made him baseball's most

#$%&'#"*#%MALIGNED#$%&#"*#%

shortstop.
His throws into the first base boxes
came less frequently
than frustrated fans
would have us believe.
He took the unjustified abuse
in good grace,
and had the last laugh
when his son became the star
he never was.

Ozzie Smith

The human vacuum cleaner.
The acrobat.
The Wizard of Oz.

Like Brooks at Baltimore,
the master of the mitt —
the incomparable one,
the magic glove —
saved more in the field
than most win with the bat.

Which is why
when the news came
we were shocked,
astounded.

It's like Santa forgetting Christmas,
Sinatra forgetting the words to "Chicago,"
Rick Barry forgetting how to shoot
underhanded free throws.
Nicklaus forgetting the way
to the clubhouse at Augusta.

Who would have thought it?
two on, two out in the ninth.
A routine grounder to end the game.

A boot.

A one in a lifetime.
The Wizard of Oz.
The goat.

Warren Spahn

Yogi's friend called him
the toughest man to face
with a runner on   THIRD
and less than   TWO
outs, and he'll be
remembered forever
because of a   SEVEN
word poem and solid
hitting and over   THREE
hundred wins
but his   FIVE
year trip to
Cooperstown was delayed
by his love of pitching

Eddie Stanky

His only talent was
his ability to win,
even if he had to kick the ball
out of the opposing shortstop's glove
to do it.

                no power
        mediocre arm
                    weak hitter
        average fielder
                    no speed

even second basemen are supposed to need more
                than nothing;

when, as manager, he couldn't turn stars
into winners, he turned to college coaching:
there, the players were as hungry
                            as he

Mel Stottlemyre

"but what have you
done for us lately?"

they asked him, the knife
hidden in one hand,
the release clear as a bell
(school's out) in the other
and ended his chance for
the World Series that he
could never pitch them
into

                    alone

Like a mistress
they don't want
you for your mind—

        at the end they
        send you out with
        the garbage
                    only
        to tell you,
        too late,
                that you
        ARE
                the garbage

Dick Stuart

RD.TNGOVESLAREG
belted the ball a

loooooooooooooooooooooooooooooooooooooooooooong

       way.

Not known for humility,
he delighted fans (hehe)
even when he made (frequent)
errors.
        Few minor league players
    ever hit
    more home runs
    in one year.
Pirate fans   loved
him   and Pirate pitchers
prayed a lot.

163

Rick Sutcliffe

Fifth and decisive playoff game, 1984:
Padres scored 4 in the seventh inning to win

It'll be a long winter, remembering
Sutcliffe in the seventh.
Faster than a cat pounces
on a daydreaming robin,
it happened.
"He did it for us all year," Frey said.
"If they beat you, make them beat your best."
Think that makes us feel better?
Platitudes and philosophy just won't wash.
We'll remember it all winter,
Sutcliffe in the seventh.

Ron Swoboda

"Did he make the sun stand still?"
(no)

"Did he make it rain for forty days?"
(no)

"Did he walk on water?"
(no)

Nothing like that,
but "'twas enough, will serve."

Even after he robbed Brooks,
management wouldn't buy the fact

that he was, without doubt,
a modern maker of minor miracles.

164

Pat Tabler

We'll always remember some clutch hits:
Bobby Thomson in 1951,
Bucky Dent in 1978,
Kirk Gibson in 1988,
Gabby Harnett in 1937,
Richie Ashburn in 1950,
Bernie Carbo and Fisk in 1975,
Cookie Lavegetto in 1947,
Chris Chamblis in 1977,
more than this page can hold.

Where is Tabler's name?
Five years from now, or ten,
will we remember him?
Maybe the greatest clutch hitter ever,
greater than Berra. Is it possible?

Tabler, with the bases loaded:
38 for 66 —
90 rbi's.
A marvel. A miracle.
A mystery
how with the sacks filled
he can deliver
at a .576 clip.

Clutch hits —
the list goes on.
Clutch hitter?
Show me one better.

Bobby Thomson

The author of:

THE WORLD'S MOST FAMOUS HOME RUN

he was destined for greatness.

Broken

bones

slowed

him

down,
and he was merely competent,
but at least he had succeeded
in making Ralph and Russ

immortal.

Marv Throneberry

The symb*l of the Mets'
early futility,
people forgot
all his home runs for Denver.
Little errors
were stretched into classic
FAUX PAS.
He drank the laughter in
like beer, perhaps
knowing, even then,
that the last laugh would be his.

The Elite of Pinch-Hitters

Burgess, Morales, and Mota were great,
And so were Greg Gross and Jerry Lynch too.
Lucas and Braun had their share of pinch-hits,
And Crowley and Kranepool had more than a few.

We can't forget Brown (the notorious Gates),
Or Mike Lum, who like Staub had a hundred or more.
Davalillo and Biittner each stroked ninety-five,
While Hairston and Dwyer banged out ninety-four.

The elite of pinch-hitters, that's what these men are.
Each one has had many a game-winning blow.
Yet their records pale beside Del Unser's feat:
For Unser hit three pinch home runs in a row.

So when you hear talk of Bevacqua or Mize,
Or they speak of Jay Johnstone or even Ty Cline,
Remind them all of what Del Unser did
With three perfect swings back in '79.

Eddie Waitkus

A

l l
u   e
b   t
e   h
l o

taught him,
        too late,
the unpredictability
of strangers in hotel
           rooms.
He helped Malamud write

The Natural

perhaps without knowing it.
He never reached the greatness
people predicted for him,
but he lived to play again.

He was more careful about
rendezvous
with
strangers.

Vic Wertz

A year before
he caught polio
like a scuffed ball,
tossed it out of play
and went on with the game,

he hit one of the longest
balls ever
(caught)

and he watched
the back of a head
for what seemed forever
until

        finally,
        finally,
        finally,
        finally,
        hat flying,
        body spinning,
        ball sailing
        into third

and he, like Mays,
became
a household
name

Hoyt Wilhelm

Paul Richards had to invent
a new glove just to catch his

  i   g   n i
w g l,n ,d c g
   g i   a   n

pitches.

Or try to.

They all mis

        s

           ed it—

the batter,
the catcher,
the umpire.

Ask umpire Red Foley:
"Ball one," he'd say.
"I know I missed it.
Don't turn around."

No one pitched
in so many games
or made so many people
so unhappy by throwing

                t

  o

                   y

s   o

     s   l

       f

Mitch Williams

*After his first game with
the Chicago Cubs*

First impressions are everything—
ask the teacher, laboring over the new student's
first written work, watching bored eyes glaze
during class discussion—

or the mother, as her daughter's first date
faces her across the doorway,
speaks in a panicked whisper—

or the baseball fan, greeting the pitcher
brought to town in place
of a traded hero.

Ask Mitch Webster in 1988 (fresh from Montreal)
how the boos lingered after that error in center
that first long day—

Now—Mitch Williams on the mound,
ninth inning, Cubs ahead 5–4;
three hits load the bases, none out,
Mike Schmidt up with 543 career dingers,
79 against the Cubs alone—
little hope now for a Sutcliffe win.

Except . . . except . . .
a whiff!
a whiff!
a . . . (can it be? can it be?) . . .
Holy Cow!
a whiff! Three in a row!
Sutcliffe wins the opener!

First impressions.
and sometimes the cheers linger
for a long
long
    while.

Ted Williams

Nothing could stop Teddy Ballgame:
not jet planes,
not steel (Splendid Splinter) shoulder pins,
not radical shifts,
not nasty (the finger) fans.
He toyed with the bat
until the pitch was on him,
thenuncoiledlikeatightlywoundspring.
Hitting is a science,
and he is Einstein.

Wilbur Wood

Looking more like a bartender
than pitcher, he floated
the knuckler toward the plate
enough times to lead the league
in both wins and losses.
Middle-aged Walter Mittys
pulled their own half-forgotten gloves
from dusty closets, exiled themselves
to suburban backyards to fling
straight knucklers to bored kids,
hoping to discover the secret
before it was too late.

Carl Yastrzemski

```
YES   he is a great player   YES
YES   who has done it all:   YES
YES   ******All-Star******   YES
YES   ****World Series****   YES
YES   ****Triple Crown****   YES
YES   **Batting Champion**   YES
YES   **Slugging Leader**   YES
YAS   *Home Run Champion*   YAS
YAS   *Defensive Standout*   YAS
YAS   Not too many players   YAS
YAS   could have replaced   YAS
YAS   a Hall of Famer as   YAS
            capably as
```

YAZ